The Social and
Religious Designs of
J. S. Bach's
Brandenburg
Concertos

The Social and Religious Designs of J. S. Bach's Brandenburg Concertos

✢

Michael Marissen

PRINCETON UNIVERSITY PRESS

PRINCETON, NEW JERSEY

Second printing, and first paperback printing, 1999

Paperback ISBN 0-691-00686-5

The Library of Congress has cataloged the cloth edition
of this book as follows:

Marissen, Michael.
The social and religious designs of J. S. Bach's
Brandenburg Concertos / Michael Marissen.
p. cm.
Includes bibliographical references (p.) and index.
ISBN 0-691-03739-6
1. Bach, Johann Sebastian, 1685–1750. Brandenburgische
Konzerte. I. Title.
ML410.B13M27   1995
784.2′4—dc20   94-28688

This book has been composed in Baskerville

The paper used in this publication meets the minimum
requirements of ANSI/ NISO 239.48-1992
(R1997) (*Permanence of Paper*)

http://pup.princeton.edu

Printed in the United States of America

1   3   5   7   9   10   8   6   4   2

For Mary
And our son, Carl

✦

Er stößet die gewaltig leben
Vom Stuhl dahin,
Und kann die Niedrigen dagegen hoch erheben.

From a cantata performed
by Bach on 2 July 1725

[God] puts down the mighty
From their thrones,
And can however exalt those of low degree.

Luke 1.52

❖ *Contents* ❖

❖ *Acknowledgments* ❖

FOR PROVIDING financial support for this project, I am grateful to the German Academic Exchange Service (DAAD), the Social Sciences and Humanities Research Council of Canada, and the Mary Albertson Faculty Fellowship committee of Swarthmore College.

For granting access to their Bach materials, I am also grateful to librarians from the former Staatsbibliothek Preußischer Kulturbesitz Berlin and Deutsche Staatsbibliothek Berlin (now reunited to form the Staatsbibliothek zu Berlin), the Musikbibliothek der Stadt Leipzig, and Princeton University. Thanks are due likewise to Reinhard Goebel, Robert Marshall, Joshua Rifkin, and Christoph Wolff for kindly making available out-of-the-way items from their personal libraries.

Of the many people who have provided criticisms and encouragement, I would like to thank especially John Butt, Eric Chafe, Laurence Dreyfus, David Lasocki, Robert Marshall, Susan McClary, Ann McNamee, Daniel Melamed, Lauren Oppenheim, Elizabeth Powers, Joshua Rifkin, Calvin Stapert, Peter Gram Swing, Emily Walhout, Christoph Wolff, and the students in the fall 1992 graduate seminar on Bach at Princeton University.

I owe the greatest debt to Mary Huissen. Her friendship and support have been invaluable, and this study is dedicated to her and to our son, Carl.

Swarthmore, Pa.
Fall 1993

The Social and
Religious Designs of
J. S. Bach's
Brandenburg
Concertos

Bach's Musical Contexts

Tubby the Tuba, at a rehearsal, sitting forlornly in the back
row of the orchestra: "Oh, what lovely music." (Sighs.)

Peepo the Piccolo, rushing to Tubby's side: "Here, what's
the matter?"

Tubby: "Oh, every time we do a new piece, you all get such
pretty melodies to play. And I? Never, never a pretty melody."

Peepo, arms stretched out: "But people don't write pretty
melodies for tubas. It just isn't done."

Paul Tripp, *Tubby the Tuba*

Tubby the Tuba captures powerfully the enculturated notion
of the orchestral hierarchy. As Tubby's story goes on to show,
there is, of course, no inherent technical reason why tubas should
not be highlighted with pretty melodies in orchestral music; it just
"isn't done." Further explanation is hardly needed.

J. S. Bach would apparently not have been moved by an appeal to
tradition. He at times assigns highly unconventional roles to the
instruments in his orchestras. To consider one of the most extreme
examples: in the alto aria from his church cantata *Du sollt Gott, deinen
Herren, lieben*, BWV 77, Bach takes the trumpet from its then conventional, D-major-trumpets-and-drums, regal, festive context and
has the instrument perform a melancholy, tortured obbligato in D
minor. To consider another extreme instance, one to be examined at
length in chapter 1: in the Sixth Brandenburg Concerto, Bach has the
violas—at the time rank-and-file, accompanimental, orchestral instruments—play brilliant solo parts, and the violas da gamba—prestigious, solo, chamber instruments—play routine, violalike accompanimental parts.

Scholars have for a long time been puzzled by such scorings. The
usual approach has been to argue that special biographical circumstances must account for them. Alfred Dürr observes that since the
idea of a trumpet obbligato seems obviously rather ill-suited to Bach's
aria text in cantata 77, there may have been external factors to ac-

count for his choice of this instrument.[1] As for the Sixth Brandenburg Concerto, Friedrich Smend provides the generally accepted explanation for its scoring.[2] He argues that whenever Prince Leopold of Köthen (Bach's employer at the time the Brandenburg Concertos were compiled) with his favorite instrument, the viola da gamba, wished to take part in the music making, Christian Ferdinand Abel, the court viola da gamba player, would of course have to move over to the second chair. If the prince took part as a soloist, it was a matter of honor for his court conductor Bach to do the same on his preferred instrument, the viola. In that case, the solo violinist in the orchestra, Joseph Spieß, would have to assume the position of second viola. The chamber musician Christian Bernhard Linigke played the cello. Bach knew how to write a piece in such a way that no excessively demanding passages were assigned to the prince, who was thus spared the embarrassment of exposing his technical limitations to his chamber musicians. The striking scorings in the Brandenburg Concertos can be easily explained: "Bach was *merely* adapting to the circumstances of performance at Köthen and the constraints imposed on him there."[3]

Dürr and Smend provide plausible enough answers to the question of why Bach's music is the way it is, but I would prefer to ask a different, if somewhat related question: what does Bach's music mean when it is the way it is?[4]

Bach's trumpet obbligato in cantata 77—or, to be more precise, his specific treatment of the instrument there—probably did in fact have something to do with internal factors. The aria text reads, "Oh, there bides in my loving still nothing but imperfection." What more effective way was there at the time to help express this imperfection than to have the natural (valveless) trumpet struggling through material that is exceedingly unnatural for the instrument?

---

[1] Alfred Dürr, *Die Kantaten von Johann Sebastian Bach*, rev. ed. (Kassel: Bärenreiter, 1985), p. 571.

[2] Friedrich Smend, *Bach in Köthen* (Berlin: Christlicher Zeitschriftenverlag, 1951), p. 24; *Bach in Köthen*, trans. John Page, ed. and rev. Stephen Daw (St. Louis: Concordia, 1985), p. 40.

[3] Smend, *Bach in Köthen*, ed. Daw, p. 41 (my emphasis).

[4] The same sorts of problems surface in research on the reception of Bach's music after his death. See Michael Marissen, "Religious Aims in Mendelssohn's 1829 Berlin-Singakademie Performances of Bach's St. Matthew Passion," *Musical Quarterly* 77 (1993): 718–26.

In the Sixth Brandenburg Concerto, Bach reverses the functions of violas and gambas, something that, as will be explained in detail in chapter 1, relates to internal aspects in the music—namely, a formal reversal in Bach's application of the syntactical properties of ritornellos and episodes in Vivaldian concerto style. The structure and scoring of Bach's concerto are significant (whatever the technical capabilities of its original players may have been), for they project alternative hierarchies to the ones accepted at the time.

One cannot, of course, prove that any sort of interpretation conveys incontrovertibly the sense of Bach's music. Considering questions of signification in Bach's concertos, however, turns out actually to be no more speculative than the generally accepted, ostensibly more straightforward idea that Bach was simply adapting to external performance constraints. Smend, for example, neither presents hard evidence leading us to conclude that Leopold would have been an incompetent gamba player nor demonstrates that Bach preferred the viola per se (the reason Bach reportedly preferred this instrument was that it put him in the middle of the harmony,[5] which means that in the Sixth Brandenburg Concerto he would probably have most enjoyed performing one of the gamba lines).

In this study of the Brandenburg Concertos, I will explore social implications both of Bach's treatment of various instruments within the hierarchical figuration of eighteenth-century court ensembles and of his handling of Vivaldian concerto style. There is nothing essentially new in this, for general observations on various sorts of analogies between politics and music were made by a great number of baroque music theorists. Volker Scherliess's research on the subject provides quotations from, among others, Athanasius Kircher's *Musurgia universalis* (Rome, 1650), Giovanni Andrea Angelini Bontempi's *Historia musica* (Perugia, 1695), Zaccaria Tevo's *Musico testore* (Venice, 1706), Johann Mattheson's *Vollkommener Capellmeister* (Hamburg, 1739), Johann Gottfried Walther's *Musicalisches Lexicon* (Leipzig, 1732), and John Hawkins's *General History of the Science and Practice of Music* (London, 1776).[6] Richard Leppert recently has argued also

---

[5] See the citations in chapter 1, n. 67.

[6] Volker Scherliess, "Musica Politica," in *Festschrift Georg von Dadelsen zum 60. Geburtstag*, ed. Thomas Kohlhase and Volker Scherliess (Neuhausen-Stuttgart: Hänssler, 1978), pp. 270–83.

along general lines for this sort of view of baroque music, and Günther Hoppe has documented Leopold of Köthen's interest in such matters.[7] John Spitzer and Neal Zaslaw, in a forthcoming book on the history of the orchestra, plan to center more specifically on contemporary understandings of the structure of instrumental court ensembles.[8] Spitzer is writing a chapter investigating the metaphors that seventeenth- and eighteenth-century writers employed to describe the orchestra,[9] and he has found that by far the most commonly used metaphors in the baroque period had to do with hierarchies, such as those of the army and of society.

In chapter 3, I will explore via his documented reading of Lutheran theology some indications that Bach himself considered the figuration of his orchestra in similar terms to the contemporary social hierarchy. Although readers may find them inherently interesting, it is probably worth exploring these nonmusical indications also on account of the powerful skepticism among many current scholars toward social interpretations of Bach's instrumental music. While any form of historical grounding is of course welcome, I would point out that the standard musicological practice of requiring proof from contemporary verbal sources (treatises, letters, etc.) for new interpretive approaches may in some sense be to take a premise for a conclusion: the practice can make it more difficult to see music itself as a formative contribution to cultural history.

All of this is not to suggest that Bach's orchestra ought to be viewed as a direct representation of society; rather, early eighteenth-century

[7] Richard Leppert, "Music, Representation, and Social Order in Early-Modern Europe," *Cultural Critique* 12 (1989): 25–55. Günther Hoppe, "Köthener politische, ökonomische und höfische Verhältnisse als Schaffensbedingungen Bachs (Teil 1)," *Cöthener Bach-Hefte* 4 (1986): 13–62, at pp. 30–31, citing Staatsarchiv Magdeburg, Abt. Köthen. A1 Nr. 22^{II}, fol. 18, which transmits a lecture pointing out correspondences between politics and music that was given during Leopold's coronation ceremonies.

[8] Zaslaw has discovered, incidentally, that the now generally accepted distinction between orchestral and chamber music did not hold in the early eighteenth century: the word *orchestra* did also clearly refer to ensembles in which there was only one player per line in the score. My thanks to Professor Zaslaw for pointing this out to me.

[9] Spitzer has presented a preliminary version of this work as "Speaking of Orchestras," 5 November 1993, national meeting of the American Musicological Society, Montreal. On this topic of orchestral metaphor more generally, see also Jacques Attali, *Noise: The Political Economy of Music,* trans. Brian Massumi (Minneapolis: University of Minnesota Press, 1985), pp. 65–67.

orchestral and social structures should both be seen as products of certain modes of hierarchical thinking.[10]

We should not assume, however, that the Brandenburg Concertos no longer "worked" at all if they were performed outside of the social contexts of the courts for which they were conceived (Sachsen-Weimar and Anhalt-Köthen) or outside of the courtly contexts for which they were revised (for Christian Ludwig, the margrave of Brandenburg in Berlin, as well as, presumably, for Prince Leopold of Köthen). In reperformances and adaptations, for example, for the bourgeois context of Bach's coffeehouse concerts or church services of eighteenth-century Leipzig (where there was no court),[11] the pieces might have lost something of their former social significance. This does mean, therefore, that the pieces never really had any such import. (In a new context, they could also even have gained other sorts of significance that they did not originally possess: for example, the musical power of Bach's dense counterpoint might have become a more striking feature for the audiences of the 1730s and 1740s, and in this context the procedures of his concertos might be considered reactionary in comparison to those then being composed according to the simpler orientation of the developing *galant* style.)

[10] On this way of looking at both society and art works as products of historical shifts in thinking and attendant behavior, see Norbert Elias, *The History of Manners* (vol. 1 of *The Civilizing Process*), trans. Edmund Jephcott (New York: Pantheon, 1978). On the structural significance of prestige in eighteenth-century Europe, see Elias, *The Court Society*, trans. Jephcott (New York: Pantheon, 1983), chap. 3, "The Structure of Dwellings as an Indicator of Social Structure."

[11] During his tenure in Leipzig, Bach arranged the first movement from an early version of the First Brandenburg Concerto as the sinfonia to the cantata *Falsche Welt, dir trau ich nicht*, BWV 52; the third movement from the First Brandenburg Concerto (or its vocal source? see chapter 1, n. 22) as the opening choruses to the cantatas *Vereinigte Zwietracht der wechselnden Saiten*, BWV 207, and *Auf, schmetternde Töne der muntern Trompeten*, BWV 207a; the third trio from the First Brandenburg Concerto as a ritornello in cantatas 207 and 207a; an early version of the first movement of the Third Brandenburg Concerto as the sinfonia to the cantata *Ich liebe den Höchsten von ganzem Gemüte*, BWV 174; and the Fourth Brandenburg Concerto as an F-major concerto for harpsichord, two recorders, and strings, BWV 1057. I will use the terms *earlier version* and *later version* for convenience but do not wish thereby to suggest that there are ideal works that undergo successively better or worse realizations. Strictly speaking, the First Brandenburg Concerto and cantata 207 do not represent different versions of one ideal musical work but are two different pieces of music with many notes and rhythms in common. Each version carries its own meanings.

One other related matter should be mentioned here. Because I have not been able to come up with a better designation, I will occasionally be using the common but unfortunate term *extramusical* to refer to the aspects of Bach's music that are concerned not simply with the notes. As the philosopher Lydia Goehr has recently reminded us, however, what we call extramusical ideals were regarded in the premodern understanding—to use standard philosophically precise terminology—as constitutive of the musical.[12] Before the nineteenth century, highly regarded music was discussed much more in terms of its functions (social, political, religious) than, as it is today, in terms of its internal, formal coherence. It was not until around 1800 that the idea of art for art's sake and the concern with individual works became regulative concepts in Western music. Goehr captures well the essentially social nature of the ongoing enterprise of finding definitions, and thereby apologia, for music: "The constant bid to define and redefine the concept of music derives from a need to convince the higher echelons of the establishment that certain musical practices are among those that are respectable and civilized. To establish the respectability of a given form of music one must make explicit what this kind of music involves as music."[13] In other words, before about 1800 what we today quite misleadingly call extramusical factors made music respectable (accordingly, instrumental music had a relatively low status), whereas after 1800, they were typically seen as a detriment to "serious" music—hence their being designated "*extra*musical" (accordingly, instrumental music achieved a relatively high status).

A FEW WORDS are in order about how this book has been organized. The central idea is that Bach's unusual treatment of instruments and handling of forms are less significant in and of themselves than in relation to one another. This premise has had certain consequences in determining which of the many possible topics surrounding the Brandenburg Concertos ought to be pursued here.[14] I have discussed

---

[12] Lydia Goehr, *The Imaginary Museum of Musical Works: An Essay in the Philosophy of Music* (Oxford: Clarendon Press, 1992), especially chap. 5, "Musical Meaning: From Antiquity to the Enlightenment."

[13] Ibid., p. 70.

[14] For more general guides to the concertos, see John Alexander Fuller-Maitland, *Bach's "Brandenburg" Concertos* (London: Oxford University Press, 1929); Peter Wacker-

organological problems, for example, only when they have immediate bearing on the interpretation of relationships between structure and scoring.[15] Thus, some consideration is given to identifying Bach's *Fiauti d'Echo* in the Fourth Concerto and classifying the violone and gamba parts in the Sixth. I did not delve into other long-standing organological issues, however, because their solution would have no bearing on the interpretive strategies adopted (e.g., the issue of whether the Fifth Concerto has anything to do with the large and expensive Mietke harpsichord Bach is known to have obtained from Berlin in 1719 is not taken up, because it would not affect the interpretation).

Similarly, I have explored only selected text-critical problems. For example, errors in the previously reported manuscript transmissions of the Sixth Concerto are pointed out in considerable detail,[16] because they directly affect the issue of Vivaldi reception in Bach. Substantial errors in the reported transmissions of other concertos go unmentioned, however, on account of their lack of relevance to the broader interpretive discussion.

Finally, I have also somewhat narrowly discussed stylistic influences on Bach's concerto procedures. As is outlined toward the beginning of chapter 1, Antonio Vivaldi played a significant role in the history of the baroque concerto by developing specific innovations in the form of this genre. Determining to what extent Bach absorbed them directly from his contact with Vivaldi's music, or secondhand through other composers, is mostly unimportant for the purposes of the interpretations explored here (Bach and his German contemporaries knew that the new formal procedures of the German concertos in the

---

nagel, *Johann Sebastian Bach: Brandenburgische Konzerte* (Berlin: Bote and Bock, 1938); Rudolph Gerber, *Bachs Brandenburgische Konzerte: Eine Einführung in ihre formale und geistige Wesensart* (Kassel: Bärenreiter, 1951); Norman Carrell, *Bach's "Brandenburg Concertos"* (London: Allen and Unwin, 1963); Elke Lang-Becker, *Johann Sebastian Bach: Die Brandenburgischen Konzerte* (Munich: Fink, 1990); and Malcolm Boyd, *Bach: The Brandenburg Concertos* (Cambridge: Cambridge University Press, 1993). Boyd's study is the most informed and insightful.

[15] A survey of organological issues in Bach research will be provided in Daniel Melamed and Michael Marissen, *J. S. Bach: A Guide to Research* (New York: Garland, forthcoming).

[16] This concerns Heinrich Besseler, ed., Johann Sebastian Bach, *Neue Ausgabe sämtlicher Werke* (*Neue Bach Ausgabe*), vol. 7, part 2: *Sechs Brandenburgische Konzerte*, Kritischer Bericht (Kassel: Bärenreiter, 1956).

1710s were Vivaldian in origin, and, in any event, they were all almost certainly familiar with Vivaldi's published concertos). And in considering relationships between scorings and structures in Bach's concertos, I have considered the role of scoring practices in other German composers to be less important than might on the face of it seem warranted. It is true that German composers personally known to Bach, like Georg Philipp Telemann and Johann Georg Pisendel, wrote Vivaldian concertos with various, even peculiar, combinations of wind, string, and brass instruments. But I considered their relevance to the present discussion of Bach to be limited, because what I took to be significant was not the mere presence of rich combinations of instruments in Bach's concertos (similar to his German contemporaries, especially in Dresden[17]) but his treatment of the scorings (rather different from the German contemporaries). That is, I viewed Bach's music to reflect less a straightforward continuation of the orchestrational practices of his native colleagues than an unprecedented critical commentary on the structures of courtly hierarchy. It seemed to me that Bach's formal indebtedness to Vivaldian models, though widely acknowledged, has been underestimated and that his orchestrational indebtedness to German contemporaries, though not so widely acknowledged, is easily overestimated.

The complex of various sorts of issues surrounding the First, Fourth, and Sixth Concertos was sufficiently wide-ranging to warrant devoting extended discussions to each of these works individually in chapter 1. Because of the more limited number of relevant problems attending the Second, Third, and Fifth Concertos, however, it was possible to discuss these works within chapter 2, which is devoted to the collection as a whole. Chapter 3 concludes by exploring the religious contexts for Bach's music as social critique.

I have been able to keep musical examples to a minimum, because it is assumed that readers will have ready access to a study score of the Brandenburg Concertos.

---

[17] This has been pointed out, for example, by Rudolf Eller, "Vivaldi and Bach," in *Studi di Musica Veneta Quaderni Vivaldiana*, vol. 1: *Vivaldi Veneziano Europeo*, ed. Francesco Degrada (Florence: Olschki, 1980), pp. 55–66; and Ortrun Landmann, "Einige Überlegungen zu den Konzerten 'nebenamtlich' komponierender Dresdener Hofmusiker in der Zeit von etwa 1715 bis 1763," *Studien zur Aufführungspraxis und Interpretation von Instrumentalmusik des 18. Jahrhunderts*, no. 20: *Die Entwicklung des Solokonzerts im 18. Jahrhundert*, ed. Eitelfriedrich Thom (Michaelstein/Blankenburg, 1983), pp. 57–73.

CHAPTER ONE

Relationships between Scoring
and Structure in
Individual Concertos

THE unquestionably vital role that "Vivaldi fever" played in the dramatic change around 1713 in J. S. Bach's compositional style is referred to regularly in recent general studies of Bach's life and works.[1] At the same time, though, investigations into this phenomenon are all too often plagued by serious analytical problems. In specialized studies on the reception of Vivaldi in Bach's concertos, for example, the usual tack has been to construct formal models for Vivaldi, against which to compare the content of Bach's music.[2] Although this approach reveals the relative richness and complexity of Bach's concertos, it has the unfortunate methodological consequence of considering Bach's concertos to be Vivaldian only when Bach's content is manifestly molded into Vivaldi's form.

---

[1] Hans-Joachim Schulze has shown by means of detailed archival research that Bach's first encounter with the new concerto style of Vivaldi's *L'Estro Armonico* collection probably took place in 1713, after Prince Johann Ernst of Weimar had forwarded to Weimar a large quantity of music purchased during his travels in the Netherlands, including, presumably, Vivaldi's *L'Estro Armonico*, published in Amsterdam a year or two earlier. See Schulze, "J. S. Bach's Concerto-Arrangements for Organ—Studies or Commissioned Works?" *Organ Yearbook* 3 (1972): 4–13; "Johann Sebastian Bachs Konzertbearbeitungen nach Vivaldi und anderen—Studien- oder Auftragswerke?" *Deutsches Jahrbuch der Musikwissenschaft* 18 (1978): 80–100; and *Studien zur Bach-Überlieferung im 18. Jahrhundert* (Leipzig: Peters, 1984), pp. 146–73. For an interesting discussion of Vivaldi's influence on Bach's compositional thinking, see Christoph Wolff, "Vivaldi's Compositional Art, Bach, and the Process of 'Musical Thinking,' " in Wolff, *Bach: Essays on His Life and Music* (Cambridge, Mass.: Harvard University Press, 1991), pp. 72–83.

[2] See, for example, Pippa Drummond, *The German Concerto: Five Eighteenth-Century Studies* (Oxford: Oxford University Press, 1980); and Martin Geck, "Gattungstraditionen und Altersschichten in den Brandenburgischen Konzerten," *Die Musikforschung* 23 (1970): 139–52. For a more sophisticated approach to formal issues, see Laurence Dreyfus, "J. S. Bach's Concerto Ritornellos and the Question of Invention," *Musical Quarterly* 71 (1985): 327–58.

Bach's concertos for an ensemble without a consistently detached soloistic subgroup represent an especially intriguing field for this sort of inquiry, because their surface stylistic features frequently tend to obscure the application of Vivaldi's ritornello procedures. For example, in the First, Third, and Sixth Brandenburg Concertos, textural and thematic contrasts are attenuated, which has led scholars to place these works outside Bach's reception of Vivaldi. In addition, the critical report in the standard scholarly edition of the concertos implies misleadingly that early versions of these pieces predate the known arrival of Vivaldi's concertos in Germany, thus providing an objective, text-critical basis for a pre-Vivaldian view of the concertos.[3] I propose to show, however, in an interpretation of relationships between structure and scoring in the First and Sixth Brandenburg Concertos, that these apparently old-fashioned ensemble works of Bach's are better understood as sophisticated responses to formal possibilities presented by Vivaldi's new concerto style and, furthermore, that Bach's procedures have interesting social implications.[4]

For the purposes of this discussion only a brief review of Vivaldian concerto style is necessary. In the concertos of Vivaldi the alternation between the tutti (entire ensemble) and the concertino (subgroup) involves contrasts in texture as well as in the type of music performed by the two groups. The tutti plays "ritornello" thematic material, and the concertino plays "episode" material. The ritornellos are expository in character, and normally they are tonally closed (i.e., they begin and end in the same key). Considered in terms of a continuum from expository to episodic, the episodes tend to be less expository in character. They are often virtuosic, and normally they begin in one key and end in another. A Vivaldian concerto movement consists mainly

[3] Heinrich Besseler, ed., Johann Sebastian Bach, *Neue Ausgabe sämtlicher Werke* (*Neue Bach Ausgabe*, hereafter *NBA*, followed by vol. and part nos.), vol. 7, part 2: *Sechs Brandenburgische Konzerte*, Kritischer Bericht (Kassel: Bärenreiter, 1956). This argument for early datings is advanced most forcefully by Geck, "Gattungstraditionen und Altersschichten." See also n. 14.

[4] Vivaldi's formal influence on the First Brandenburg Concerto is discussed in Hans-Günter Klein, *Der Einfluß der Vivaldischen Konzertform im Instrumentalwerk Johann Sebastian Bachs* (Strasbourg: Heitz, 1970), pp. 52–56; and Peter Ansehl, "Genesis, Wesen, Weiterwirken: Miszellen zur Vivaldischen Ritornellform," *Informazioni e Studi Vivaldiani* 6 (1985): 74–85 (the excerpts concerning Bach are reprinted in Ansehl, "Zum Problem der Ritornellstrukturen in den Brandenburgischen Konzerten von Johann Sebastian Bach," *Cöthener Bach-Hefte* 4 [1986]: 96–100).

of free episode material with occasional returns of part or all of the ritornello. In fact, Vivaldi's specific contributions to the development of the Venetian baroque concerto were to make opening tuttis tonally closed and to intensify the stabilizing function of the tuttis by employing literal or transposed quotations from all of the now easily separable segments in the opening tutti. By contrast, in the concertos of Vivaldi's predecessors often only the head of the first—tonally "open"—tutti would return in the course of a movement, whereas the continuations—also tonally open, save the final one—might employ different thematic material in each instance.[5] The rationality of Vivaldi's formal innovations probably goes a long way in helping explain why Vivaldi's concertos evidently appealed to Bach so much more than the concertos of Vivaldi's predecessors.

In his concerto-style works Bach shows a predilection for a Vivaldian ritornello type containing three clearly differentiated segments, a type that falls within the category of what modern German-speaking students of Vivaldi's music have labeled the *Fortspinnungstypus* ("spinning-forth type," or "fortspinnung-type"). In the fortspinnung-type ritornello favored by Bach, the first segment grounds the tonality with primarily tonic and dominant harmonies, ending on either the tonic or the dominant (more typically the dominant). The second segment follows with sequential thematic material whose harmonic rhythm is marked mostly by root movement by fifths. And the third segment, whether involving further sequencing or other procedures, brings the ritornello to a satisfying close by way of a cadential gesture in the tonic.[6] For an example of a Vivaldi ritornello clearly structured along these lines, see the opening ritornello in the third movement from his E-major violin concerto, Op. 3, no. 12 (RV 265; cf. Bach's arrangement of this piece for keyboard solo, BWV 976), as illustrated in example 1, where the points of division occur at mm. 7 and 17.

Writers in various languages still refer to the three segments of this particular variety of fortspinnung-type ritornello with the German

---

[5] On the baroque concerto and Vivaldi's specific formal contributions to the genre, see Michael Talbot, "The Concerto Allegro in the Early Eighteenth Century," *Music and Letters* 52 (1971): 8–18, 159–72.

[6] On formulating these categories primarily in terms of harmonic properties rather than thematic ones, see Dreyfus, "J. S. Bach's Concerto Ritornellos."

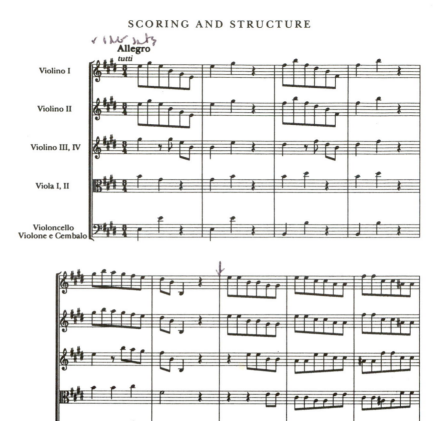

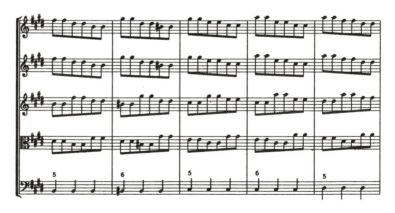

Example 1. Vivaldi, Concerto in E major, RV 265, third movement

Example 1, *continued*

terms *Vordersatz, Fortspinnung,* and *Epilog.*[7] I will use "fortspinnung-type" to describe only this specific variety of Vivaldian ritornello.[8] And because there do not appear to be any fully satisfactory translations for *Vordersatz, Fortspinnung,* and *Epilog,* I will treat them as English words, much like *kindergarten* and *gesundheit*—or, for that matter, like the Italian word *ritornello.*

THE FIRST BRANDENBURG CONCERTO

The opening movement of the First Brandenburg Concerto certainly has none of the obvious external features of the new Vivaldian concerto form.[9] The Vivaldi concertos that Bach transcribed for keyboard in the early 1710s were scored for violin (or violins) and string ensemble, and they featured relatively clear textural and thematic contrasts between the ritornellos and the episodes. Bach's concerto, on the other hand, is scored for several choirs of instruments (two horns, three oboes with bassoon, and string ensemble), and its continually changing subgroups do not necessarily coincide with contrasts in thematic material. On the face of it, the scoring and the style appear to have more in common with German ensemble music of earlier decades than with the Vivaldian string concertos that had become modish in Saxony by the time Bach sent his dedication score of the Brandenburg Concertos to the margrave of Brandenburg (in 1721). The German Bach scholar Martin Geck, for example, associates the opening movement of the First Brandenburg Concerto stylistically

[7] These terms are derived from similar ones employed in Wilhelm Fischer, "Zur Entwicklungsgeschichte des Wiener klassischen Stils," *Studien zur Musikwissenschaft* 3 (1915): 24–84.

[8] At times Bach scholars also use the term *Fortspinnung-type ritornello* for ritornellos with other sorts of spinning forth than sequencing (e.g., sixteenth-note figures repeated at the same pitch level), as well as for ritornellos without initial segments having the properties described above under the term *Vordersatz.* See, for example, the discussions of the arias "Jagen ist die Lust der Götter" and "Schafe können sicher weiden" from *Was mir behagt, ist nur die muntre Jagd!* BWV 208, and "Er segnet, die den Herrn fürchten" from *Der Herr denket an uns,* BWV 196, in Miriam K. Whaples, "Bach's Earliest Arias," *Bach* (the journal of the Riemenschneider Bach Institute) 20, no. 1 (1989): 31–54, at pp. 35, 39, 45. See also Alfred Dürr, *Studien über die frühen Kantaten Johann Sebastian Bachs: Verbesserte und erweiterte Fassung der im Jahr 1951 erschienenen Dissertation* (Wiesbaden: Breitkopf and Härtel, 1977), pp. 123–24, 172.

[9] A slightly different version of this discussion has appeared as "Concerto Styles and Signification in Bach's First Brandenburg Concerto," forthcoming in *Bach Perspectives* 1 (1995).

and chronologically with the instrumental overtures to German sacred vocal works of the late seventeenth and early eighteenth centuries, especially those of Friedrich Wilhelm Zachow (1663–1712), who scores several of his cantatas with horns, oboes, and strings.[10] But as Geck's colleague Rudolf Eller has more recently pointed out, Vivaldian concertos scored with similar combinations of wind instruments were cultivated decades later by composers at the Dresden court, during Bach's lifetime.[11] That is, Geck's concern with the dating of the First Brandenburg Concerto and his comparison with Zachow will initially appear compelling more on the questions of contrapuntal styles than on the scorings or forms.

Consider how Bach organizes the opening thirteen measures in this movement. He structures mm. 1–6 with vordersatz, fortspinnung, and epilog segments (closing, however, on the dominant); mm. 1–3 emphasize the tonic and dominant triads, mm. 3–4 feature sequential material, and mm. 4–6 approach a clearly defined cadence. A second and third fortspinnung segment follow: in mm. 6–10 the oboe and string families proceed, separately in mm. 6–7 and then together in mm. 8–10, with sequential material loosely derived from the vordersatz segment. The design concludes with a second and third epilog: mm. 10–13 twice lead to a cadence on the tonic (first deceptive, then authentic). Hereafter I will refer to this series of segments with the abbreviations V–Fa–Ea–Fb1–Fb2–Eb1–Eb2. Because various permutations of segments from this tonally closed block of material are used during the course of the movement (in most cases more than once),[12] mm. 1–13 and the returns would correctly be viewed as modeled, thematically and tonally, on the new Vivaldian fortspinnung-type ritornello procedure.

Texturally, however, mm. 1–13 do not correspond at all to the Vivaldian procedure. Bach engineers a reduction in the scoring toward the middle of the ritornello (from full ensemble with horns, to oboe and string families together, to oboe and string families alternating). He also designs a buildup of the scoring toward the close (from

[10] Geck, "Gattungstraditionen und Altersschichten," 145.

[11] Eller, "Vivaldi and Bach," in *Vivaldi Veneziano Europeo*, ed. Francesco Degrada, Studi di Musica Veneta Quaderni Vivaldiana (Florence: Olschki, 1980), vol. 1, pp. 55–66.

[12] See mm. 21–24 (Fa–Ea), 27–33 (V–Fb2–Eb1), 43–48 (V–Fb2–Eb1'), 52 (part of V), 57 (part of V), and 72–85 (entire ritornello).

oboe and string families alternating, to oboe and string families together, to full ensemble with horns). Furthermore, m. 13 does not mark the entrance of a soloist or soloists with entirely new thematic material but initiates alternating full-ensemble and subgroup textures with thematic material obviously derived from mm. 1–6 of the ritornello. Measures 13–15 emphasize the tonic and dominant triads, mm. 16–17 proceed sequentially, and mm. 17–18 approach a close on the dominant. In other words, Bach structures this block too with vordersatz, fortspinnung, and epilog segmentation. Because this syntactically ritornellolike block of material (hereafter "episode 1") does recur (see mm. 58–63), it could be thought of as a second (though, in this case, tonally open) ritornello.

Owing to an exact tonal and thematic correspondence to Fb1 in mm. 6–8, the section from mm. 18–19a will initially be experienced as a return of a segment from the "first ritornello." This is the case even though the textural contrast occurs in the wrong direction (the episode of mm. 13–18 closes in full-ensemble texture with horns, and m. 18 commences with only the string group). In mm. 19b–21 Bach alters and extends the sequence of mm. 6–8, however, and closes on F major. Thus, although the segments of episode material in mm. 13–21 modulate from the tonic to the dominant and touch on both the supertonic and the submediant, the episode closes back at the tonic. Bach breaks this potential tonal monotony in m. 21 with a subdominant ritornello featuring the initial Fa and Ea segments (see mm. 3–6), performed by the tutti minus the horns.

The run of mm. 1–24, then, appears to be strikingly at odds with the stylistic premises of the Vivaldian string concerto. The one palpable trace of this concerto style lies in the subsequent literal quotation of thematic material with internal vordersatz, fortspinnung, and epilog segmentation. The textural and thematic contrasts conform rather less closely to Vivaldian expectations.

Properly contrasting and modulating episodes arrive in mm. 24–27 (hereafter "episode 2") and mm. 33–36 (hereafter "episode 3"), both featuring alternating quasi-Corellian textures (i.e., two treble lines and continuo: from horns and continuo, to the first two oboes and continuo, to violins and continuo).[13] A more extended episode at

---

[13] Arcangelo Corelli's concertos represent a different Italian concerto tradition from the Venetian. Corelli's concertos rarely feature thematic contrasts between tutti and

mm. 36–43 (hereafter "episode 4") is scored for the full ensemble, thereby allowing Bach to turn Vivaldi's textural contrast on its head: the ritornello of mm. 43–48 has a thinner texture and sonority than the previous (blasting) episode for horns, oboes, and strings.

The complexity of the formal and contrapuntal relationships encountered in mm. 1–24 is nowhere relieved in the rest of the movement. For one thing, Bach has each of the subsequent episodes come back as well (episode 2, mm. 48–52 and 53–57; episode 3, mm. 63–65; and episode 4, mm. 65–72). What is more, all the episodes are ultimately derived from the thematic material of the opening ritornello. Episode 1, as mentioned earlier, opens with thematic material from the beginning of the ritornello (cf. mm. 13–18 and 1–6) and continues with thematic and tonal material based on the Fb1 ritornello segment of mm. 6–8; the continuo of episode 2 adopts the falling sequence of ascending tetrachords in the continuo line of Fb1 but adds new counterpoint in the treble; episode 3 takes from episode 2 the treble line and the ascending tetrachords of the continuo but inverts and extends them; episode 4 adopts the descending version of the tetrachord but presents it in augmentation (see horn 1, mm. 36–37a) above a continuo line adapted from the treble counterpoint of episode 3. From this outline, it should be clear that each of the latter three episodes is based on some novel feature of the episode that precedes it and that, consequently, the episodes gradually distance themselves thematically from the ritornello.

Throughout the movement these five blocks of related material (the ritornello and the ritornello-derived episodes 1–4) are juxtaposed with each other. Since all this material returns, everything in the movement is, strictly speaking, "ritornello." A composer's proceeding in this unusual and limiting manner could easily yield an

---

solo; they concentrate rather on textural contrasts of the same thematic material, typically between the tutti and a subgroup of two violins and continuo. There is no evidence that Corelli's concertos were known outside of Rome before they were published in 1714. For example, Vivaldi's incorporation of Corellian features in some concertos in *L'Estro Armonico* stems not from an independent study of Corelli but from the influence of Giuseppi Valentini's Op. 7 concertos published in 1710 in Bologna; see Michael Talbot, "Vivaldi and Rome: Observations and Hypotheses," *Journal of the Royal Musical Association* 113 (1988): 28–46, at p. 28. That Bach had direct knowledge of Corelli's trio-sonata style is attested to by his B-minor organ fugue, BWV 579, which is based on the fourth sonata from Corelli's Op. 3.

uninteresting concerto movement. Yet there is nothing dull or inevitable about the form of Bach's concerto, for the ordering of the blocks of material is unpredictable. This is not to say that Bach's compositional procedure is haphazard, for he may have planned out his various returning segments in this seemingly arbitrary way specifically to contravene the regularity of his Vivaldian models, works in which segments of the same ritornello more predictably punctuate ever-changing episode material.

The opening movement of Bach's First Brandenburg Concerto, then, can be viewed as a rigorous, complex, and sophisticated manifestation of the formal possibilities presented by Vivaldi's mercurial, simple, and flamboyant new concerto style. Bach's methods of shaping the tonal and thematic material in this movement are no doubt indebted to his encounter in the early 1710s with Vivaldi's *L'Estro Armonico* concertos. Yet at the same time his carefully worked out architectural approach to the whole, with its involved contrapuntal procedures and step-by-step moving away from the ritornello in its episodes, is essentially foreign to Vivaldi's more spontaneous style. In fact, Bach reintroduces the very kind of complexity that the Italian concerto style had presumably been admired for avoiding.

According to the interpretation offered here, Bach both expands and contracts a Vivaldian model. Whereas the Vivaldian model assumes a two-way contrast between an expository fortspinnung-type ritornello for the ensemble and episodic material for the soloists, Bach creates a structure with a five-way contrast between a fortspinnung-type ritornello, a fortspinnung-type episode, and, finally, three only somewhat less expository episodes, two of which (1 and 4) are scored for full ensemble. And, while Vivaldi assumes a contrast between a continually returning ensemble ritornello and mostly new episodes, all of Bach's material returns throughout the movement, and all of it is related thematically. Bach appears interested not merely in the binary opposition of ritornello and episode but also in the notion of relative episodic distance from the ritornello. He does not simply fill a Vivaldian formal model with complex or more developed content; he develops the model itself—and in a way that, unlike Vivaldi concertos, does not readily lend itself to mass production. In this singular concerto movement Bach appears antithetically to complete his predecessor by retaining some of the original terms but assigning them different meanings. By this procedure Bach realized the inherent formal potential of the new concerto style much more fully than Vivaldi's equally enthusiastic but more literal German imitators.[14]

An alternative explanation might be that Bach adopted the vorder-satz-fortspinnung-epilog syntax found occasionally in the opening tuttis of some pre-Vivaldian concertos but, in contrast to the procedures of those pieces—in which initial tuttis are not tonally closed and subsequent tuttis often do not quote the opening fortspinnung and epilog segments, providing new material instead—decided to make his opening tutti tonally closed and have all his material, including the episodes, return in literal quotations later in the movement. Accordingly, Bach's procedure for his literally quoted, tonally closed ritornellos would be not actually Vivaldian but rather the logical by-product of a fusion of ideas taken from the pre-Vivaldian concerto for strings and the blocklike permutation fugue for keyboard or for voices. A fundamental problem with this explanation, though, is that the vordersatz-fortspinnung-epilog syntax—leaving aside whether it is tonally closed or whether its specific thematic material is quoted subsequently in the movement, in the Vivaldian manner—does not appear in any of Bach's works that can be securely dated to before about 1713.

HAVING EXPLORED Bach's unique approach to Vivaldian concerto procedure in the opening movement, we now have a meaningful context in which to consider questions of signification through his unusual treatment of early eighteenth-century instruments.

[14] Johann Georg Pisendel and Prince Johann Ernst of Weimar, to name two. We should note also that the nonmusical evidence provided to support the prevalent view that the first movement from the First Brandenburg Concerto was conceived at an early (pre-Vivaldian) point in Bach's career (the dating suggested by Geck) turns out to be rather weak. Following Johannes Krey, "Zur Entstehungsgeschichte des ersten Brandenburgischen Konzerts," *Festschrift Heinrich Besseler zum sechzigsten Geburtstag*, ed. Institut für Musikwissenschaft der Karl-Marx-Universität (Leipzig: VEB Deutscher Verlag für Musik, 1961), pp. 337–42, many Bach scholars maintain that an earlier version of the First Brandenburg Concerto probably served as a sinfonia for the cantata *Was mir behagt, ist nur die muntre Jagd!* BWV 208, a work that, according to Dürr, ed., *NBA* 1.35: *Festmusiken für die Fürstenhäuser von Weimar, Weißenfels und Köthen*, Kritischer Bericht (1964), pp. 39–43, was in existence by early 1713 (Krey mistakenly believed Bach composed the cantata in 1716); Yoshitake Kobayashi, "Diplomatische Überlegungen zur Chronologie der Weimarer Vokalwerke" (paper delivered at the Bach-Kolloquium Rostock, 1990), accepts Dürr's Kritischer Bericht but has suggested that this date might even be moved back to 1712. But it turns out that the arguments in support of Krey's cantata-sinfonia hypothesis are marred by serious factual errors. On this issue, which involves too many

The participation of two *Corni di caccia* (hunting horns) in a concerto grosso must have seemed unusual to early eighteenth-century audiences, for in the 1710s and 1720s the hunting horn was by no means a standard member of instrumental ensembles with strings. Furthermore, there are no known German precedents for the participation of horns in a concerto.

The horn first achieved stature in connection with the mounted hunt.[15] The size and grandeur of a nobleman's hunt became a symbol of his wealth and social status, for the expenses associated with the hunt were enormous. He had to purchase and maintain a respectable number of horses and hounds, weapons, musical instruments (one could live for a year on the price of a horn!), uniforms, and so on. Large amounts of money were paid to individuals who could play the horn as well as ride and shoot.

Just like the hunt reflected a nobleman's social standing, so did the horn become a status symbol within the hunt. The musical skill of the mounted horn players came to be almost as important as their prowess in the field. Their elaborate systems of hunting calls turned the musical aspect of the hunt into a magnificent showpiece for their patron.

Beyond the strong associations with aristocracy and the outdoor life of the privileged classes, the hunt also embodied contemporary moral and philosophical principles. The mounted hunt ceremony was well suited for adoption into aristocratic life at the end of the seventeenth century, a time when the ancient courtly ideals inherited from the middle ages were seeking forms of expression more in line with the worldliness and prosperity of the late baroque. The hunt was emblematic of *Tugend* (worldly virtue; a complex mixture of bravery, industry, honesty, and chivalry), signifying a new manifestation of the older *ritterlich-höfisch* (chivalrous-courtly) ideals central to aristocratic thought. Owing to its ceremonial and signal functions in the hunt, the horn emerged as an allegorical figure representing aristo-

---

details for inclusion here, see Michael Marissen, "On Linking Bach's F-Major Sinfonia and His Hunt Cantata," *Bach* 23, no. 2 (1992): 31–46. Incidentally, there is also no secure evidence that Bach composed instrumental concertos of any sort before his encounter with Vivaldi's.

[15] I have taken this account of the horn's place in the hunt and its affective connotations from Horace Fitzpatrick, *The Horn and Horn-Playing and the Austro-Bohemian Tradition from 1680–1830* (London: Oxford University Press, 1970), 16–21.

Example 2. Bach, First Brandenburg Concerto, first
movement, horn, mm. 1–2
Contemporary hunting-horn signal

cratic values. The sound of the horn was therefore able to excite deep
feelings in the aristocracy, in whose minds it symbolized the very essence of nobility.

Because of these associations, the original effect of horns in early
eighteenth-century concerted music was probably much more evoca-
tive than we might suspect today. The fanfares in Reinhard Keiser's
Octavia of 1705 provide an early example of the coloristic employment of horns for evoking the salubrity of the outdoors and the grandeur of aristocratic life. And in the "Quoniam" of Bach's B-minor
Mass the horn's affective connotations highlight the image of God's
entry into the world as a human being in the form of Christ the king.

To return to the First Brandenburg Concerto: in conjunction with
the various returning episode blocks that are gradually less dependent thematically on the ritornello, it is possible to chart significant
patterns in Bach's handling of the *Corni da caccia* within the first
movement.

In the opening ritornello, Bach assigns the horns their traditional
role, going so far as to quote literally a greeting call familiar to contemporary Saxon huntsmen (see example 2).[16]

[16] This greeting call, as given in example 2, is illustrated (without citing its source) in
Fitzpatrick, *The Horn and Horn-Playing*, p. 20; it is not found among the (few) horn
signals printed in Hanns Friedrich von Fleming, *Der vollkommene Teutsche Jäger* (Leipzig,
1719), vol. 1, pp. 311–12. There can be little doubt that Bach is quoting a hunting call,
for the flourish appears in a number of other places; Fitzpatrick, *The Horn and Horn-
Playing*, pp. 60–62, for example, suggests Bach may have come across it in Johann
Joseph Fux's overture to the ballet music he set for Marc'Antonio Ziani's opera *Me-
leagro*. The same fanfare, scored for horn, has regal associations in the aria "Der Herr
ist König ewiglich" from *Lobe den Herrn, meine Seele*, BWV 143 (for the purposes of the
present discussion, questions regarding the authorship of this cantata are unimportant); see Charles Sanford Terry, *Bach's Orchestra* (London: Oxford University Press,
1932), p. 46. The fanfare also appears with the same associations, this time scored for
trumpet, in the aria "Grosser Herr und starker König" from part 1 of Bach's Christmas
Oratorio as well as in the earlier version of this aria, "Kron und Preis gekrönter Damen"

But this is no genteel transfer of hunting-field music into the salon. Beyond considering the visual sensation that these outdoor instruments would probably have made inside the small and elegant chamber music rooms used by Bach's ensemble, it is worth examining more closely the aural impression that they create within the structure of the First Brandenburg Concerto. In the ritornello, the horns clash rather strongly with the rest of the ensemble, by means of three-against-four rhythms (mm. 2–3, 8–10, and 12) and conflicting harmonies (m. 12). (Apparently disturbed by these conflicts, many conductors today instruct their horn players to perform the ritornello as quietly as possible.) The rest of the ensemble, a choir of oboes and a choir of strings, cooperates closely in the ritornello, either proceeding essentially in unison or alternating with briefer gestures. Thus, by the very calling up of their traditional, aristocratic associations, the horns disrupt the surface order of Bach's otherwise complete, double-choir ritornello. And, in spite of their striking presence, the horn parts could be removed from the ritornello without affecting its formal coherence or contrapuntal integrity.

Just as the episodes gradually become less dependent thematically on the ritornello, so the horn writing for these episodes gradually becomes less akin to the idiomatic horn writing of the ritornello. Already in the episode of mm. 13–18 (episode 1) the horns move away from their hunting signals in favor of material loosely related at first to the oboe figuration of the vordersatz segment. For the remainder of the episode, the horn parts stay thematically distinct from the ritornello-derived material of the accompanying string and oboe choirs. Nonetheless, the presence of the horns remains unessential to the structure. That is, here, as in the ritornello, the horn lines could be removed without any formal or contrapuntal damage (apart, perhaps, from the second half of m. 14). When the horns do become contrapuntally and formally essential, in m. 20, they no longer dissociate themselves from the rest of the ensemble but instead participate in the refined alternation of group gestures familiar from the second fortspinnung segment of the ritornello (Fb1, mm. 6–8). This gradu-

---

from *Tönet, ihr Pauken, Erschallet, Trompeten*, BWV 214; see Edward Tarr, "Monteverdi, Bach und die Trompetenmusik ihrer Zeit," in *Bericht über den internationalen musikwissenschaftlichen Kongress Bonn 1970*, ed. Carl Dahlhaus (Kassel: Bärenreiter, 1971), pp. 592–96, at p. 595. More curious is the fanfare's (slightly altered) appearance in the string parts to Gavotte II from Bach's Orchestral Suite in C major, BWV 1066.

ally approached assimilation with the material shared by the rest of the ensemble is then maintained in episodes 2 and 3 (mm. 24–27 and 33–36), where treble pairings of horns, oboes, and violins alternate with the same episode material. The return of episode 3 in m. 53 carries this instrumental assimilation even farther by pairing the treble instruments from different choirs. The process borders on caricature in episode 4 (mm. 36–43): proceeding at first in dissonant fourth-species counterpoint—a style of writing entirely foreign to eighteenth-century brass instruments[17]—the horns for the first time assume unambiguously the principal voice throughout an entire episode. As in the ritornello, they are strikingly differentiated from the ensemble, but, unlike in the ritornello, they are now contrapuntally indispensable.

Although these procedures might be attributed wholly to Bach's musical ingenuity or rational inclination, it is difficult to ignore their social implications. Just as the episodes only gradually gain a formal identity by becoming less dependent on the ritornello, the horns lose their social identity by becoming gradually assimilated into the more neutral instrumental style of the rest of the ensemble. That is, the string and oboe choirs are not contrasted by violinistic or oboistic treatment; instead both choirs play counterpoint that is not instrument-specific. And the horns reach their greatest prominence contrapuntally only when, at the end of the process, they adopt a style utterly unidiomatic to the instrument. (As if in recognition of having gone too far, Bach closes this episode with more conventional clarino-style writing; see mm. 38–43.)

This bridging of the social distance between the horns and the rest of the ensemble in the First Brandenburg Concerto would have been more readily apparent to the early eighteenth century's musical connoisseurs than today's, who are likely to be unaware of the configuration of performing organizations in Bach's time. In this work, Bach juxtaposes three groups of instruments (the pair of horns, the oboe choir, and the string choir) that are somewhat disparate from a social

---

[17] To my knowledge, the only (somewhat) similar example from roughly contemporary brass parts occurs in the trumpet parts to the first chorus of Bach's cantata *Wir danken dir, Gott, wir danken dir*, BWV 29 (more familiar from Bach's later versions as the "Gratias" and "Dona nobis pacem" in the B-minor Mass, BWV 232; note, however, that this entire chorus is in *stile antico*). Later examples include the opening period of Mozart's Piano Concerto in E♭ major, K. 482.

perspective. In the way Bach initially uses them, the horns would doubtless have been associated with the nobleman's mounted hunt, thus referring to a rather high social status within the musical hierarchy. Bach's string choir would have been most readily associated with the ripieno of the court instrumental ensemble, pointing up a respectable status within the hierarchy but one beneath the horns and the other soloists within the court instrumental ensemble (court soloists carried the distinguishing title of *Cammermusiker* and were paid a much higher salary than musicians who were used only as ripienists). The oboe choir might have been associated with military bands or with the *Stadtpfeifer* (municipal musicians), reflecting a respectable status within the musical hierarchy but one somewhat lower than that of court musicians.[18]

In this interpretation, instead of employing various families of instruments merely for their coloristic effect, Bach worked out a concerto movement in which implied social associations for the instruments are brought into significant relationships via an unorthodox application of Vivaldian ritornello procedure. By means of this relationship between scoring and structure, Bach is able to achieve in music what was not possible in the real world: by having the groups within the ensemble of his concerto movement gradually function as and thus become equals, Bach neutralizes social distinctions that at the time would normally have been taken for granted. It was therefore perhaps not fortuitous that Bach in Leipzig placed this movement at the head of a church cantata contrasting the world's speciousness with God's loyalty (*Falsche Welt, dir trau ich nicht*, BWV 52): the aristocratic elements become the world's vainglory.

There are, of course, many eighteenth-century pieces in which the instruments are treated equally, but I am not aware of any other com-

---

[18] Although sometimes there was a *Cammermusiker* in the court ensemble who played the oboe, court conductors would have had to engage city musicians in the uncommon event that a piece required as many as three oboes. On the social position of the oboe in the eighteenth century, see Werner Braun, "The 'Hautboist': An Outline of Evolving Careers and Functions," in *The Social Status of the Professional Musician from the Middle Ages to the Nineteenth Century*, ed. Walter Salmen (New York: Pendragon Press, 1983), pp. 132–33. Court conductors would also have had to engage city musicians in the unlikelihood that a piece required a large ripieno string section. The musically respected *Stadtpfeifer* and related *Kunstgeiger* employed for cantata performances by Bach in his subsequent tenure at Leipzig had no *Cammermusiker* to compete with, for Leipzig was not a court city.

poser than Bach who manipulates instrumental writing gradually, that is, in such a socially significant way. Other composers, like Telemann and Vivaldi, either employ instruments equally from the start in a way that does not seem socially significant or else use them unequally in a manner that, if interpreted socially, would reflect rather than challenge uncritically held social assumptions.

IF THE INTEREST in the opening movement centers on the horns and their relationship to Bach's application of Vivaldian concerto procedure, the focus in the remaining movements shifts to the role of the violino piccolo (a small violin, tuned in this case a minor third higher than the normal violin). As with the discussion of the first movement, I will consider formal aspects before interpreting Bach's scoring socially in terms of court-ensemble figuration.

In assembling this version of the concerto, Bach appears to have designed only the third movement with the violino piccolo in mind from the start. There is no part whatever for the instrument in the early version of the work (the Sinfonia BWV 1046a, formerly BWV 1071), which lacks both the third movement and the Polonaise.[19] In the Brandenburg version, the violino piccolo line is mostly borrowed note for note from the first violin part of the early version. The violino piccolo doubles the first violin in the opening movement and in the tutti minuet of the Brandenburg version. And in the second movement, Bach gives to the violino piccolo what was originally the first violin part of the early version and writes new filler material for the first violin. (The instrument is not called for in any of the three trios to the minuet.)

The violino piccolo thus plays a marginal role in the first movement. The only place it is independent from the first violin part is in mm. 54–57. The instrument is here neither a real soloist (thus contra-

[19] Perhaps I should point out that the earliest surviving manuscript for the Sinfonia BWV 1046a (Mus. ms. Bach P 1061, Staatsbibliothek zu Berlin, copied by Christian Friedrich Penzel in 1760), strictly speaking, does not transmit the early version of the First Brandenburg Concerto. Rather, as Ulrich Siegele explained already in his 1957 dissertation for Tübingen University (published as *Kompositionsweise und Bearbeitungstechnik in der Instrumentalmusik Johann Sebastian Bachs* [Neuhausen-Stuttgart: Hänssler, 1975]), the Sinfonia BWV 1046a, the Sinfonia from cantata 52, and the First Brandenburg Concerto are all revised versions separately based on the lost original; the Sinfonia BWV 1046a, however, is apparently the only version preserving Bach's original sequence of movements (see Siegele, *Kompositionsweise*, pp. 146–50).

dicting the *concertato* in Bach's title for the margrave of Brandenburg's score[20]) nor an integral member of the ripieno ensemble. In the second movement—a sort of triple-concerto movement in which the first oboe, the violino piccolo, and the continuo instruments constitute the concertino—the violino piccolo is a true member of the concertino; yet it is the first oboe that gets treated as if it were the central soloist in the ensemble: see the cadenza in m. 34.

To focus briefly on other aspects of the second movement, consider that in slow movements in Italian concertos ornamented melodies are presented in an extended episode that is typically set against two tutti statements almost perfunctorily opening and closing the movement.[21] In this slow movement, however, Bach dispenses with a framing tutti and opens directly with highly ornamented melody (played initially by the first oboe), placed in a passacaglialike setting. And, whereas in Italian concertos the solo melody has a quasi-improvisatory character, Bach's ends up far from improvisation: it gets subjected to sophisticated contrapuntal treatment in the form of a quarter-note canon at the unison (see mm. 12–14 and 23–25). Here, then, is a further indication—to add to those already pointed out in the first movement—that the First Brandenburg Concerto is a far more complex composition than its Italian models.

Only in the third movement does the violino piccolo seem to have achieved the function of central soloist. But even here its status appears problematic when the relationship between Bach's scoring and his structure is explored.[22] The opening tutti comes as close as one

[20] 'Concerto 1mo á 2 Corni di Caccia. 3 Hautb: è Bassono. Violino Piccolo concertato. 2 Violini, una / Viola è Violoncello, col Basso Continuo.'' Staatsbibliothek zu Berlin, Am.B.78. Facsimile: Peter Wackernagel, ed., *J. S. Bach, Brandenburgische Konzerte: Faksimile nach dem im Besitz der Staatsbibliothek in Berlin befindlichen Autograph* (Leipzig: Peters, 1947).

[21] For an example of a Bach concerto following this pattern, see the slow movement of the E-major harpsichord concerto, BWV 1053.

[22] Bach used this movement again, in D major, as the opening choruses to his secular cantatas *Vereinigte Zwietracht der wechselnden Saiten*, BWV 207 (in 1726), and *Auf, schmetternde Töne der muntern Trompeten*, BWV 207a (in the 1730s). Malcolm Boyd, *Bach: The Brandenburg Concertos* (Cambridge: Cambridge University Press, 1993), pp. 61–70, makes a strong case for the suggestion that the two cantata choruses and the concerto movement may have originated in some still earlier vocal composition in F major, now lost. According to Boyd, this would help to explain the unusual nature of Bach's writing for the violino piccolo and the movement's somewhat unusual structure. Attempting simply to account for Bach's use of a small violin tuned a third higher than the ensemble, Andreas Moser suggests that the piece may have been composed for a performance

will get in the Brandenburg Concertos to textbook Vivaldi ritornello structure.[23] It consists of vordersatz (mm. 1–4; hereafter "V"), a double fortspinnung segment (mm. 5–7 and 8–11; "F1" and "F2"), and a double epilog (mm. 12–15 and 15–17; "E1" and "E2"). The first episode, mm. 17–20, is modeled very closely on the V segment of the ritornello. The second episode, mm. 25–35, consisting of two extended sequential passages, is related thematically to the F1 and F2 segments of the ritornello. And the brief third episode, mm. 38–40, provides a clear cadence in the newly established tonality. Considered collectively, the three episodes conform rather closely to the syntax of the opening ritornello (opening statement, two consecutive sequences, and a cadence). In fact, when joined together in a continuous series, mm. 17–20, 25–34, and 39–40 form a musically coherent entity. If these episodes are labeled with lowercase letters to indicate their affinity with the segmentation of the ritornello, the run of mm. 1–53 could be summarized as V–F1–F2–E1–E2 / v / V / f1–f2 / V / e / F1–F2–E1–E2.

Although in the first episode the violino piccolo adopts material that is closely related to the head of the ritornello's V segment, the instrument attempts to distinguish itself through virtuosic multiple stops in every measure. It continues to strive in this manner through the return of the V segment in mm. 21–24. Bach even instructs all the other members of the ensemble here to play *piano sempre* and *pianissimo sempre*, presumably to ensure that they will not drown out the chords of the (solo) violino piccolo. In the second episode, the vio-

---

by Bach's oldest son, Wilhelm Friedemann, who was only a child at the time and therefore perhaps too small to handle a normal violin; see Moser, "Der Violino piccolo," *Zeitschrift für Musikwissenschaft* 1 (1918–19): 377–80. It is common among Bach scholars to attribute his unusual writing either to lost originals with different scorings or to special biographical circumstances. The inference from this approach, it often seems, is that we are relieved, partly if not entirely, of having to come to terms with such works in the form in which we know them. I would not contest the observations that from the formal point of view the opening choruses of cantatas 207 and 207a seem much less unusual than the third movement of the First Brandenburg Concerto, or that Bach may have been accommodating a particular player with the concerto's solo violin part. In interpreting relationships between Bach's scorings and structures, I am, strictly speaking, seeking not to account for how Bach's concertos came to have their forms but rather to consider the meanings they project in the forms that they have (on this issue, see the introduction).

[23] Although scholars have generally considered the first movement to be un-Vivaldian, they agree on the Vivaldian style of the third movement.

lino piccolo is overshadowed first throughout f1 by the first oboe and the first violin and then throughout f2 by the first horn. So in spite of a great deal of flailing by the violino piccolo—the instrument at this point has even thicker textures than in the first episode, with numerous triple stops and even one quadruple stop—it does not quite emerge as a genuine soloist presenting its own thematic material. It does stand out properly for the first time in the third episode, where it has its own material and is accompanied only by the continuo, but here it turns out that the apparently purposive move of cadencing in the dominant may be formally redundant. If this two-measure, interruptive solo were removed, the concerto would proceed, beginning in m. 35, with a syntactically complete quotation of the ritornello in the dominant (V–F1–F2–E1–E2).

The violino piccolo abandons the syntax of the fortspinnung-type ritornello and presents its own thematic material for its episodes in the B section of this da capo movement (mm. 53–83). Nonetheless, its solo status remains problematic. Right at the outset, in mm. 53–55, the first oboe and the two horns appear to remind the violino piccolo of its straying from the true path of the ritornello, as it were, by providing in the (*piano*) accompaniment fragmentary quotations from the V segment of the ritornello. Coming out of this, the first oboe immediately assumes the principal voice in a trio-sonata texture with violino piccolo—marked by stock pathetic gestures of slurrings by twos—and continuo (mm. 55–60). And, with its fragmentary V and f1 quotations, the ensemble, particularly the horns, completely overshadows the violino piccolo in a second approach to the A-minor cadence (mm. 60–63). On the other side of the A-minor ritornello (F2–E1; mm. 63–70), this procedure recurs in reverse order (mm. 70–80), with one subtle difference: in the passage of trio-sonata texture, the first violin part assumes the principal voice (mm. 74–80), thus approximating the timbre of the struggling violino piccolo soloist.[24] And Bach marks the first violin part of the ensemble "pia[no]" at m. 74 even though he had already marked this part "p[iano]." at m. 70. He seems intent

[24] The Brandenburg Concertos were probably performed with one player per line in the score. See Marissen, "Performance Practice Issues that Affect Meaning in Selected Bach Instrumental Works," in *Perspectives on Bach Performance*, ed. Robin Stowell (Cambridge: Cambridge University Press, forthcoming). Many performers today use multiple players on the ripieno violin 1 line and thus possibly obscure the sense of this passage.

on having the solo violino piccolo line, which again is merely a secondary voice consisting primarily of stereotypical slurred couplets, performed more loudly than the principal voice.

At m. 82 it appears that the violino piccolo will finally achieve some semblance of its long-denied genuine solo status. Bach's fermatas in all parts except the violino piccolo and his Adagio marking provide the traditional context within concerto style for the improvised cadenza, a prerogative belonging to the soloist. But by the violino piccolo's third note in the mini-Adagio the ensemble appears already to be bringing the written-out cadenza to a quick close. The continuo adopts specifically the hemiola rhythm and the intervallic content of the closing (epilog) segment of the ritornello. In this interpretation, a performance will best reflect the sense of the cadenza by accelerating from the second half of m. 82 until the initial tempo of the movement is resumed in the second half of m. 83. (Note in this connection that neither the double bar nor the Allegro indication found at m. 84 in several modern editions appears in Bach's own score.[25])

The structure of the seven dances following the Allegro is a quasi-symmetrical one in which a tutti minuet contrasts with trios performed by various subsets of the ensemble. Bach designates them as "Menuet—Trio á 2 Hautbois è Bassono. Corni è Viole tacet.—Menuet—Poloinesse. Tutti Violini è Viole. mà piano. Violino piccolo tacet.—Menuet—Trio à 2 Corni & 3 Hautbois in unisono—Menuet." Having explored several Italian concerto styles in the first three movements, Bach now turns from the Italian style altogether by presenting a series of French, Polish, and German dances. He does not entirely abandon concerto principles, however, for the continually returning tutti minuet acts as a sort of ritornello in relation to the three trios with reduced textures.

For these dances the violino piccolo resumes the marginal role in the ensemble that it had taken on in the opening movement of the concerto. In fact, Bach appears to have organized the style of the dances to emphasize this diminished role. In the ritornello (the tutti minuet), the violino piccolo merely doubles the first parts in the string and oboe choirs. The style of the tutti minuet conforms closely

---

[25] Interestingly, this passage, and what precedes it, reads differently in the choral versions of the movement.

to the French court minuet, which was designed for dancing in carefully prescribed step patterns (note the characteristic two-bar phrases and the twelve- rather than sixteen-bar strains).[26] In keeping with the French style, Bach sets the first trio as a minuet for the first and second oboes and bassoon, a scoring commonly referred to today as the "Lullian trio." The second trio is a polonaise, an aristocratic Polish dance, scored for the string choir, minus violino piccolo, and the continuo group. And the third trio is a piece of Germanic hunt music scored for the two horns (constituting the upper two parts) and the three oboes playing in unison. It is worth pointing out that in court dances only individuals of the highest status were given the privilege of comprising the smaller groups who danced the trios while the larger group looked on. Intriguingly, in Bach's series of dances all the instruments except for the putative soloist (the violino piccolo *concertato*) have an opportunity to participate in trios while the ensemble looks on.

The trio most likely to have included the violino piccolo is the string-choir polonaise, the center of Bach's seven-movement dance series. Bach appears to have composed the polonaise at around the same time that he copied the new version of this concerto for the margrave of Brandenburg,[27] and therefore he could very easily have accommodated a violino piccolo part. Even as the trio stands it would require changing only a few low notes in m. 28 to make the first violin line playable on the violino piccolo. (Bach had made similar changes for the instrument in the first two movements of the concerto.) Perhaps it was because of this very ease of adaptation that Bach went to the trouble of inserting "Violino piccolo tacet" below the title to the trio. His similarly squeezed-in "Tutti" indication between "Poloinesse" and "Violini è Viole" further emphasizes the exclusion of the violino piccolo.

---

[26] For specific information on the step patterns in the French minuet, see Meredith Ellis Little, "Minuet," in *The New Grove Dictionary of Music and Musicians*, ed. Stanley Sadie (London: Macmillan, 1980), vol. 12, pp. 353–58. See also nn. 91–92 here.

[27] The Polonaise is not fully autograph, which suggests that Bach had recently composed the movement and therefore did not need to copy the music himself. (In the opening movements, presumably composed somewhat earlier, he would have wanted to do the copying himself so that he could immediately enter revisions as he went along.) On the identification of the nonautograph handwriting, see Georg von Dadelsen, *Beiträge zur Chronologie der Werke Johann Sebastian Bachs* (Trossingen: Hohner-Verlag, 1958), p. 84.

In connection with this apparent snubbing of the soloist for a Polish dance movement, there is evidence that German musicians of the day considered the violino piccolo to be a Polish instrument. The following comments on Polish tavern music appear in the Telemann autobiography that was published in 1740:

> When the court [of Count Erdmann von Promnitz at Sorau (now Zary in Poland)] removed to Pless [now Pszczyna] for six months, one of Promnitz's estates in Upper Silesia, I heard there, as I had done in Cracow, the music of Poland and the Hanaka region of Moravia in its true barbaric beauty. In the country inns, the usual ensemble consisted of a violin strapped to the body and tuned a minor third higher than ordinary, which therefore could out-shriek half a dozen normal violins; a Polish bagpipe [an instrument made of goatskin with the head, horns, and all left intact on the bag]; a trombone; and a regal [a small portable organ with snarling reed pipework]. In respectable places, however, the regal was omitted and the number of the first two instruments listed was increased; in fact, I once heard thirty-six [Polish] bagpipes and eight [piccolo] violins playing together. One would hardly believe the inventiveness with which these pipers and fiddlers improvise when the dancers take an intermission. An observer could collect enough ideas in eight days to last a lifetime. But enough; this music, if handled with understanding, contains much good material. In due course I wrote a number of grand concerti and trios in this style, which I clad in an Italian coat with alternating Allegri and Adagi.[28]

At any rate, if Bach did associate the violino piccolo with Poland, its exclusion from the only Polish movement in the concerto is nothing if not ironic.

The violino piccolo seems also to have been excluded, in a less obvious manner, from the final trio. In the early version of the con-

---

[28] This translation is adapted slightly from the one found in Richard Petzoldt, *Georg Philipp Telemann*, trans. Horace Fitzpatrick (New York: Oxford University Press, 1974), p. 25. For the original, see Johann Mattheson, *Grundlage einer Ehren-Pforte* (Hamburg, 1740), quoted in Werner Rackwitz, ed., *Georg Philipp Telemann: Singen ist das Fundament zur Music in allen Dingen—Eine Dokumentensammlung* (Leipzig: Philipp Reclam jun., 1981), p. 202.

certo, BWV 1046a, the trio is scored for two horns, with the lowest line written for violins instead of oboes. Bach appears to have composed the oboe version of the trio at the last minute, for in the margrave's dedication score the music to this trio is not in Bach's handwriting,[29] suggesting that he had just composed it and therefore did not need the copying process as an opportunity for on-the-spot entering of minor revisions, something he would more likely have wanted if the piece were one he had pulled from his drawer of older pieces.[30] Because it is far from clear that one version represents a compositional improvement over the other, Bach may have had some other reason to go to the trouble of writing the alternative version—such as to ensure the participation in the trios of every player from the ensemble except the violino piccolo (remember that the other violins had already played in the polonaise and that the third oboe had not yet appeared in a trio).

The treatment of Bach's "Violino Piccolo *concertato*" throughout the concerto takes on additional interest when his scorings and structures are interpreted socially. A *concertato* part for solo violin would have been most readily associated in the early eighteenth century with the principal violinist in the court instrumental ensemble. In reference to the ensemble he would have carried the designation *Konzertmeister* (concert master), or in reference to the group of *Cammermusiker* he would have enjoyed a title like *Premier Cammermusicus*.[31] The *Kapellmeister* (conductor) was typically the only person in the court musical establishment to receive a higher salary.[32] Accordingly, the solo violin enjoyed a relatively elevated status within the court ensemble. In this concerto, Bach appears to be deflating this status both quite literally

---

[29] This is pointed out in Dadelsen, *Beiträge zur Chronologie*, p. 84.

[30] Furthermore, a close look at the trio's heading, which is in Bach's hand, reveals that the ampersand between "2 Corni" and "3 Hautbois in unisono" may have been carefully revised from an uppercase *V*, suggesting that Bach initially intended to copy out the version of the trio with the "Violini" (hence the *V*). But it seems unlikely that Bach would at the first instance have omitted a conjunction or a period between "Corni" and "Violini."

[31] This was the title, for example, of the violinist Joseph Spieß, the concertmaster at the Köthen court while Bach was employed there; see Besseler, *NBA* 7.2, Kritischer Bericht, p. 20.

[32] The only musicians who might have been better remunerated than a *Kapellmeister* were opera singers. At those few courts that boasted opulent opera establishments, the (mostly foreign) singers were paid fabulous sums, often well more than ten times what an average *Konzertmeister* received.

by writing for "Violino *piccolo* concertato" and musically by preventing the violino piccolo *concertato* from achieving true solo character. To recapitulate: in the opening Allegro, the violino piccolo merely doubles the first violin part; in the slow movement, it constitutes only one member of a group of soloists drawn from the ensemble; in the third movement, it vainly strives for independence from the ensemble or fails to sustain being the principal voice when it is independent; and in the dances, it either merely doubles the soprano voice of the ensemble or remains silent in places where its presence would most readily be expected.[33]

The First Movement
of the Sixth Brandenburg
Concerto

Though the Sixth Brandenburg Concerto is widely considered to represent one of Bach's earliest instrumental works, it appears here too that, as with the first movement from the First Brandenburg Concerto, an apparently old-fashioned ensemble work of Bach's can upon closer examination be understood as a sophisticated response to formal possibilities presented by Vivaldi's new concerto style.[34]

As mentioned at the outset, it is well established in studies of Bach's music that the year 1713 marks a dramatic change in his compositional style and that this style change can be attributed largely to Bach's having become acquainted with Vivaldi's concertos; and, as also mentioned, Bach appears to have been especially intrigued by the fortspinnung-type ritornello as it was developed in Vivaldi's

---

[33] Eric Chafe describes the progression from movement to movement as a dialectical one, proceeding from the unusually pompous and external opening movement, to the unusually plaintive and inward slow movement, to the synthesis in the third movement where both the full court ensemble and the violino piccolo as central soloist are heard for the first time; see Chafe, *Tonal Allegory in the Vocal Music of J. S. Bach* (Berkeley and Los Angeles: University of California Press, 1991), p. 182.

[34] Slightly different versions of this discussion have appeared as "Relationships between Scoring and Structure in the First Movement of Bach's Sixth Brandenburg Concerto," *Music and Letters* 71 (1990): 494–504, and "Beziehungen zwischen der Besetzung und dem Satzaufbau im ersten Satz des sechsten Brandenburgischen Konzerts von Johann Sebastian Bach," *Beiträge zur Bach-Forschung* 9–10 (1991): 104–28. I first worked out this interpretation in a paper for the spring 1982 proseminar in musicology taught by Laurence Dreyfus at Washington University.

new concerto style. This fortspinnung-type ritornello begins to surface immediately not only in Bach's concertos but also in his vocal works as well as his keyboard preludes and even fugues. Three examples from outside Bach's concertos, illustrated in examples 3–5, are relevant for discussing the Sixth Brandenburg Concerto. First, the closing chorus from the cantata *Christen, ätzet diesen Tag*, BWV 63, which, as an interesting hybrid example, contrasts modern, fortspinnung-type ritornellos in the orchestral interludes with more old-fashioned, motetlike episodes in the choral writing (mm. 1–3 of the opening ritornello are a vordersatz segment, mm. 3–5 are fortspinnung, and mm. 5–8 are epilog; motet-style writing starts in m. 13). Second, the Prelude from the English Suite in G minor, BWV 808, for solo harpsichord (mm. 1–8 of the opening section are a vordersatz segment, mm. 8–23 are fortspinnung, and mm. 23–33 are epilog). And finally, the Fugue in D major, BWV 532, for solo organ (mm. 1–2 of the subject are a vordersatz segment, mm. 2–5 are fortspinnung, and mm. 5–6 are epilog).[35]

Considering next mm. 1–21 of the first movement of the Sixth Brandenburg Concerto, we will find it difficult to discern any similarity of structure between the concerto excerpt and each of the three indicated examples from Bach's vocal and keyboard works. The internal organization of the concerto excerpt up to the cadence (at m. 17) will defy description in terms of the fortspinnung-type ritornello (and in fact the rambling, thematically homogeneous character of this extended material is foreign to all types of concerto ritornello). Furthermore, the tonic cadence does not mark the entrance of a soloist or subgroup, for the entire ensemble keeps playing. On the face of it, the scoring (a small, somewhat unusual combination of six low stringed instruments) and the writing (a two-voiced canon at the eighth note and, after the tonic cadence, a five-voiced canon at the half note) would appear to have more in common with seventeenth-century church sonatas than with ensemble concertos of 1721, the date marked on Bach's dedication score to the margrave of Brandenburg. Bach's fellow German composers were celebrating the avoidance of this contrapuntal complexity as they caught "Vivaldi fever" during the second decade of the eighteenth century.

[35] On other stylistic grounds, George B. Stauffer, *The Organ Preludes of Johann Sebastian Bach* (Ann Arbor: UMI Research Press, 1980), p. 108, dates the Fugue BWV 532 to the (pre-Vivaldian) period c. 1706–12.

Example 3. Bach, *Christen ätzet diesen Tag*, BWV 63, closing chorus

Example 3, *continued*

Example 3, *continued*

Example 3, *continued*

Example 3, *continued*

41

Example 3, *continued*

Example 3, *continued*

Example 3, *continued*

44

Example 3, *continued*

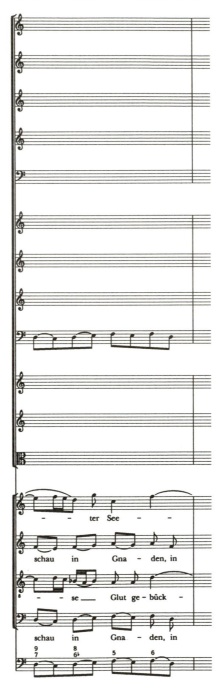

Example 3, *continued*

Example 4. Bach, English Suite in G minor, BWV 808, Prelude

Example 5. Bach, Fugue in D major, BWV 532

It should therefore hardly be surprising that many students of Bach's music still consider the Sixth Brandenburg Concerto to be one of Bach's earliest instrumental works: its surface traits differ strikingly from those of the concertos of his contemporaries.[36]

But it is worth considering carefully the section between the first and the second cadences (i.e., mm. 17–25). This material divides into three parts, and the thematic characteristics of each of the divisions correspond exactly to those of the Vivaldian fortspinnung-type ritornello. The three examples from Bach's vocal works and solo keyboard works mentioned in the preceding showed that it would be misguided to require a study of Vivaldi reception in Bach to restrict itself to examining such obvious places as the opening tuttis of orchestral concertos (i.e., those three works exhibit Bach's employing Vivaldi's fortspinnung-type ritornello procedure in motet, suite, and fugue—all somewhat unlikely places for the application of such a model). It appears, then, that in the ostensibly old-fashioned Sixth Brandenburg Concerto the first few bars following the tonic closure of the extended block of opening material (i.e., the place where the first episode appears in a Vivaldian concerto) neatly fit the description of a vordersatz segment (mm. 17–21), the next few bars of fortspinnung (mm. 21–23), and the cadencing bars of epilog (mm. 23–25).[37]

What Bach has succeeded in effecting for the first two sections of his concerto movement, then, is a reversal in the applications of the thematic syntax typically found in the first two sections—ritornello/episode—of a Vivaldi concerto.[38] Bach provides an extended tutti section (mm. 1–17) in which there are no internal points of syntactical

[36] The most sustained argument for this prevalent view has been advanced by Geck, "Gattungstraditionen und Altersschichten," pp. 139–52.

[37] Klein, *Der Einfluß der Vivaldischen Konzertform*, p. 47, n. 11, points to the fortspinnung-type segmentation of initial episodes in the first movement of Bach's A-minor violin concerto, BWV 1041; the first movement of the Fifth Brandenburg Concerto; the first movement of the Sixth Brandenburg Concerto; the first and third movements of the E-major harpsichord concerto, BWV 1053; and the first movement of the C-major concerto for two harpsichords, BWV 1061.

[38] One might argue that, despite the frequent use of fortspinnung-type syntax in concerto ritornellos, linking these two things for the interpretive purposes explored here is, strictly speaking, arbitrary: fortspinnung-type syntax merely provides a way of getting from one musical point to another. Although this observation at first, in the abstract, may seem compelling, it is presumably significant that in historical practice, fortspinnung-type syntax is rarely encountered outside of ritornellos or initial episodes (whether in concertos, arias, choruses, sonatas, or keyboard preludes); that is, composers must have considered the syntax to provide an especially satisfying way of getting from specific kinds of points to others, most notably those that mark off ritornellos.

division (cf. the rambling character of many Vivaldian episodes). And this is followed by a thinning-out modulatory section (mm. 17–25) in which there are three points of division conforming to the characteristics of fortspinnung-type syntax (cf. the segmentation of many Vivaldian ritornellos). In Bach's concerto, however, the categories are still able to retain their functional identities, for the opening material comes in a contrapuntally dense, full-ensemble texture and displays tonal closure (i.e., therefore it would still warrant being called a ritornello), whereas the subsequent material begins in another contrapuntally dense, full-ensemble texture before its second half thins out to a *Bassätchen* texture and modulates to the dominant (i.e., therefore it would still warrant being called an episode).

Having securely set up the two functions, Bach can extend this reversal during the course of the movement by having the opening ritornello modulate at its second appearance (mm. 25–28) and by having the first episode (mm. 17–25), which begins in the tonic and ends in the dominant, return with tonal closure (mm. 32–40; see also mm. 65–73 and 103–14). In other words, even though Bach's reversals of the conventional characteristics of ritornello and episode are extreme, the question of identifying individual sections later in the movement as ritornello or episode is not confusing. Instead of adhering to the external conventions or laws of concerto form (i.e., where certain syntactical, textural, and tonal properties match up), Bach has structured the peculiar opening of the Sixth Brandenburg Concerto to allow the work to set up its own rules internally.[39]

[39] An interesting parallel example of this sort of systematic reversal of modern formal conventions clothed with the external features of an older genre is found in Bach's F-major organ toccata, BWV 540. The piece opens with material that is related on the surface to the manual *passaggio* and pedal solo of the traditional North-German organ prelude. But in Bach's toccata the figuration is not free and rhythmically irregular; rather, the thematic contours are triadic and rigidly motoric (i.e., Vivaldian). Furthermore, the manual passagework is organized as a strict canon, and the pedal solo is derived from the canon. After this prefatory material, the toccata develops into a concerto movement in which continually returning full-textured modulating sections alternate with continually returning reduced-textured, more expository, nonmodulating sections that are derived from the manual canon and pedal solo. Here, in other words, as in the Sixth Brandenburg Concerto, Bach effects a systematic reversal of Italian concerto procedures. Compare the interpretations of this toccata in Stauffer, *The Organ Preludes*, pp. 46–51, and Dominik Sackmann, "Toccata F-dur (BWV 540)—eine analytische Studie," in *Bericht über die wissenschaftliche Konferenz zum 5. Internationalen Bachfest der DDR*, ed. Winfried Hoffmann and Armin Schneiderheinze (Leipzig: VEB Deutscher Verlag für Musik, 1988), pp. 351–60.

Bach also injects into the structure a viola solo (mm. 40–45), accompanied chordally by the full ensemble but behaving in a thematically and tonally correct manner (like in Vivaldi, it contrasts with the
ritornello by being episodic in character and modulatory; also, it is
not contrapuntally dense). This constitutes a third kind of event in
the concerto movement. By its lack of complex counterpoint, this episode strongly distinguishes itself texturally from the surrounding material. But, unlike in the majority of Vivaldi's episodes, where the thematic material is clearly differentiated from tutti sections, Bach's viola
solo material is derived from the previous vordersatz segments of his
fortspinnung-type episodes (compare mm. 17–18 with mm. 40–41).
By this means Bach effects a further attenuation of Vivaldian syntax.

It is worth mentioning that the potential for another sort of reversal
is only rarely realized in performances of the first movement of the
Sixth Brandenburg Concerto. Without an explicit tempo marking in
Bach's score to follow, ensembles, perhaps overwhelmed by the seri-
ousness of the counterpoint and the dark scoring, tend to play the
movement rather slowly. An Allegro tempo is called for, however,
both by the cut-time signature and by the fact that the movement is
the first of a three-movement concerto that, as it appears from close
examination, does employ the syntax of Vivaldi's concerto style. We
should also note that the opening movements of the vast majority of
Bach's instrumental works do not carry a tempo indication, unless
something other than a simple Allegro is desired.[40] In a properly
quick tempo, the ritornellos in the first movement of the Sixth Brandenburg Concerto will give a slightly more virtuosic impression than
the episodes.

The first movement of Bach's Sixth Brandenburg Concerto, then,
can be viewed, like the first movement of the First Concerto, as a
rigorous manifestation of the formal possibilities presented by
Vivaldi's flamboyant new concerto style. Bach's methods of structur-
ing and shaping the tonal and thematic material in this movement are
no doubt indebted to his encounter with Vivaldi's *L'Estro Armonico*
concertos. Yet at the same time it is difficult to imagine how both the

---

[40] See Robert L. Marshall, "Tempo and Dynamic Indications in the Bach Sources:
A Review of the Terminology," in *Bach, Handel, Scarlatti: Tercentenary Essays*, ed. Peter
Williams (Cambridge: Cambridge University Press, 1985), pp. 259–75, at pp. 270–71;
this essay has been reprinted in Marshall, *The Music of Johann Sebastian Bach: The Sources,
the Style, the Significance* (New York: Schirmer, 1989), chap. 15.

broad outlines of the form and the details of the content could be more different from Vivaldi.

Comparing Bach strictly to a formal model constructed for Vivaldi, we could be misled by the archaic appearance of the surface stylistic features of this movement. The absence of strong textural contrasts between orchestral ritornellos and soloistic episodes might suggest that the piece represents a striking counterexample for the study of Vivaldi reception in Bach and even that the piece is not really a concerto at all.[41] But according to the interpretation that I have been outlining, Bach at the same time expands and contracts a Vivaldian model in this piece. Whereas Vivaldi assumes a two-way contrast between continually returning fortspinnung-type orchestral material and ever new episode material, Bach creates a structure with a three-way contrast between thematically unsegmented ritornellos, fortspinnung-type episodes, and, finally, more conventional episodes. Furthermore, all three return throughout the movement, feature the entire chamber ensemble, and share related motivic cells. Once again, Bach does not merely fill a Vivaldian formal model with complex or more developed content. He develops the Vivaldian model itself.

ALTHOUGH some of the most recent research on Bach chronology places the Sixth Brandenburg Concerto before Bach's earliest encounter with Vivaldi's concertos, the text-critical evidence in fact supports a dating consistent with the interpretation of the concerto as a sophisticated example of Vivaldi reception.

In the critical report accompanying his edition of the Brandenburg Concertos for the *Neue Bach-Ausgabe,* Heinrich Besseler claimed that two early manuscript copies of the concerto, a score and a set of performing parts, share some distributed errors as well as a number of minor variant readings.[42] He concluded that the one copy was dependent on the other and that the manuscripts could have been derived from the readings of an earlier autograph score. Believing the Sixth Concerto to be the earliest of the Brandenburg Concertos, Bes-

---

[41] See, for example, Norman Carrell, *Bach's "Brandenburg Concertos"* (London: Allen and Unwin, 1963), p. 23: "[Brandenburg Concerto] No. 6 is, in the author's opinion, not a concerto of any kind."

[42] Besseler, *NBA* 7.2, Kritischer Bericht, pp. 143–44.

seler placed its composing score at around 1718 on stylistic grounds unrelated to Vivaldi reception,[43] but subsequent research has argued that this lost score could have come from a much earlier point in Bach's career.[44]

Martin Geck has bolstered the argument for an early origin by suggesting that for the outer movements Bach expanded the scoring of a (now lost) earlier work, adding the viola da gamba parts around 1721.[45] He based this conclusion on the presence of a number of corrections in the gamba parts in the margrave's dedication score and on the absence of corrections in the viola parts. Noting, moreover, what he perceived to be a lack of Vivaldian concerto-style traits in the piece, Geck concluded that Bach had conceived the work as a trio sonata at a very early point in his career, well before Vivaldi's concertos became known in Germany. Geck reasoned that because with the Fifth Brandenburg Concerto Bach had probably exhausted his usable store of concertos, he decided to close the set with an orchestrated trio sonata rather than compose a new concerto for the margrave.

Naturally the implications of Besseler's and Geck's text-critical reports, to the extent that they favor an early placement of the Sixth Brandenburg Concerto in the chronology of Bach's works, do not sit well with an interpretation of the piece as a study in Vivaldi reception. The piece certainly cannot be said to develop Vivaldi's concerto procedures if it was composed before Vivaldi's concertos reached Bach.

As regards Besseler's score and set of parts, an examination of these materials reveals that the distributed errors he cites are simply not there. Furthermore, Besseler's shared variant readings distinguishing the two manuscripts from the readings of the margrave's dedication score were not there originally. They are performance markings that were clearly entered in the nineteenth century, when both manuscripts were associated with Carl Friedrich Zelter and the Berlin Singakademie. And finally, the score and the set of parts are in fact dependent on the margrave's score.[46]

[43] Besseler, "Zur Chronologie der Konzerte Joh. Seb. Bachs," in *Festschrift Max Schneider zum achtzigsten Geburtstag*, ed. Walther Vetter (Leipzig: VEB Deutscher Verlag für Musik, 1955), pp. 115–28; see also his comments in *NBA* 7.2, Kritischer Bericht, pp. 23–28.

[44] See especially Geck, "Gattungstraditionen und Altersschichten," pp. 139–40.

[45] Ibid., pp. 147–48.

[46] The text-critical details are provided here in appendix 1.

About the revisions to which Geck was referring for the gamba parts in the margrave's score, it should be pointed out that the changes are not signs of compositional activity but merely corrections of entries that had been copied a third too low.[47] Taking into consideration the fact that the parts are notated in the tenor clef,[48] one could conclude from the consistency of the corrections that Bach's exemplar was a score with the gamba parts notated conventionally in the alto clef.

Indications of a previous score with alto clefs in all four upper parts might, on the other hand, suggest an earlier version for the similarly unusual scoring of four violas. Consider, for example, the sinfonia to Bach's cantata *Gleichwie der Regen und Schnee vom Himmel fällt*, BWV 18, which, in its Weimar version, is scored for four violas and continuo. But in the original performance parts to the cantata (Mus. ms. Bach St 34, Staatsbibliothek zu Berlin; Bach's score is lost), only violas 1 and 2 are notated in the alto clef, while violas 3 and 4 are notated in the tenor clef. The cantatas *Christ lag in Todesbanden*, BWV 4; *Weinen, Klagen, Sorgen, Zagen*, BWV 12; *Der Himmel lacht! die Erde jubilieret*, BWV 31; *Widerstehe doch der Sünde*, BWV 54; *Aus der Tiefen rufe ich, Herr, zu dir*, BWV 131; *Erschallet, ihr Lieder, erklinget, ihr Saiten!* BWV 172; and *Himmelskönig, sei willkommen*, BWV 182, also have viola parts that were notated in the tenor clef in the original materials.[49] Except for the parts in the margrave's dedication score of the Sixth Brandenburg Concerto, the only Bach gamba part notated in the tenor clef in the eighteenth-century manuscripts is the second gamba line in the early copy, apparently apograph, of the cantata *Gottes Zeit ist die allerbeste Zeit*, BWV 106, and its notation alternates between tenor and bass clefs.[50] Since Bach wrote gamba and viola parts in tenor and alto clefs, we cannot draw conclusions about the scoring of Bach's exemplar for the margrave's score of the Sixth Brandenburg Concerto from the clef indications by themselves. In any case, it would be extremely unlikely for Bach to have made a number of transposition errors from a score for four violas in alto clefs and

[47] For the text-critical details, see appendix 2.

[48] Laurence Dreyfus, *Bach's Continuo Group: Players and Practices in His Vocal Works* (Cambridge, Mass.: Harvard University Press, 1987), p. 167, erroneously reports that Bach set the gamba parts in the Sixth Brandenburg Concerto in the alto and tenor clefs.

[49] See Ulrich Prinz, "Studien zum Instrumentarium Johann Sebastian Bachs mit besonderer Berücksichtigung der Kantaten" (Ph.D. diss., Tübingen University, 1979), p. 72.

[50] Ibid., p. 99.

not have made any visible compositional revisions—especially, for example, in the places where the gamba parts go below the range of the viola.

The question of why Bach would bother to shift gamba parts in the alto clef to the tenor clef remains. He may have done so in order to heighten visually the distinction specified with his "Viola da Braccio" and "Viola da Gamba" headings for the margrave's score. (Similarly fastidious copying procedures, presumably also motivated by visual concerns, are found for several other concertos in the margrave's dedication score.[51])

It is clear, then, that text-critical evidence cannot be used to challenge a dating of the Sixth Brandenburg Concerto to after 1713, for, as a close examination of the early manuscripts shows (see appendix 1), the margrave's dedication score transmits the earliest surviving readings. It should be at the top of the stemma for the transmission of the concerto. Although I see no obvious reason, for instance, why the Sixth Brandenburg Concerto could not have been among Bach's very latest concertos written in Köthen,[52] I do not feel compelled to suggest a specific dating, for my concern centers on exploring Bach's reception of Vivaldi's concerto form as something inherently interesting, not on the use of style criticism for dating works whose composing scores are lost.

BACH'S REMARKABLE reversal of Vivaldian formal syntax in the first movement is paralleled in reversals of conventional roles for the instruments. This is apparently the only concerto in the history of the genre scored for two violas, two violas da gamba, cello, violone, and continuo harpsichord. The grouping of these instruments in an ensemble creates a striking visual impression, for it sets up a contrast of lower-pitched members of the violin and viola da gamba families.

In early eighteenth-century German baroque music, violas and cellos were normally treated as standard ripieno instruments in orchestral scorings. Their function was basically accompanimental, and so they were usually given relatively easy parts to play. Only rarely

[51] See the discussions of the atypical notations of the Fourth and Fifth Concertos here at pp. 68–69 and p. 106, n. 73, respectively.

[52] There is nothing about the scoring, either, to preclude a later dating; see the discussion cited at the end of n. 61.

were they given important solo parts. Gambas, on the other hand, were normally treated as special instruments in chamber scorings. Their function was basically soloistic, and so they were usually given rather difficult parts to play. Bach's treatment of the instruments in the Sixth Brandenburg Concerto is significant: the violas and cello press forward with virtuosic solo parts, while the gambas amble along with easy ripieno parts. In other words, as a formal correlative to his reversal of the conventional thematic characteristics of ritornellos and episodes, Bach also reverses the conventional functions of the instruments.[53]

One might object that this interpretation of the Sixth Brandenburg Concerto is speculative (understood pejoratively), for there is a simpler and more mundane way of understanding this work: the concerto would have been designed for a particular ensemble in which the viola players (e.g., Bach) were technically more accomplished than the gamba players (e.g., Prince Leopold of Köthen). But whatever the concerto's unusual scoring and structure might signify is not necessarily altered one way or the other by identifying its original players.[54] Also (leaving aside its failure to consider Bach's structural reversals), I would say that the mundane view of the concerto, though not implausible, is equally speculative. There is no hard evidence to suggest that Leopold would have been an incompetent gamba player: the eighteenth-century writer Johann Adam Hiller reports, for example, that Leopold was a respectable singer and violinist.[55] And any court "Chamber Musician upon the Gamba" (like Christian Ferdinand Abel at Köthen) would, of course, by definition have been a talented player. Furthermore, in the eighteenth century, any musician with virtuoso viola technique was normally a violinist (the idea of the concert violist postdates the eighteenth century), and so if it had been simply a matter of Bach's being forced to accommodate instrumental

---

[53] Another symptom of this sort of role reversal is found with Bach's solo cello suites, BWV 1007–12. As Laurence Dreyfus has pointed out, Bach went out of his way to compose suites for the cello in the absence of any tradition and wrote sonatas for the gamba and obbligato harpsichord (BWV 1027–29); given the historical position of both instruments, cello sonatas and gamba suites would seem a more plausible assignment. See Dreyfus, ed., *Joh. Seb. Bach: Drei Sonaten für Viola da Gamba und Cembalo BWV 1027–1029* (Leipzig: Peters, 1985), "Concluding Remarks," p. 63.

[54] See also n. 22.

[55] Johann Adam Hiller, *Lebensbeschreibungen berühmter Musikgelehrten und Tonkünstler, neuerer Zeit* (Leipzig, 1784), p. 135.

proficiency, he would much more likely have written the piece for the less unconventional scoring of violins and gambas.

It should not be assumed, incidentally, that Bach never writes virtuosic solo viola parts or easy ripieno gamba parts. See, for example, the difficult viola solo in the cantata *Wo soll ich fliehen hin*, BWV 5, and the ripieno gamba parts in the choruses of the "Trauerode" (*Laß, Fürstin, laß noch einen Strahl*), BWV 198. What is interesting about the Sixth Brandenburg Concerto is that both these exceptional uses of the instruments are placed in a striking relationship to each other. Bach's virtuosic treatment of the viola in one piece or his orchestral treatment of the gamba in another piece might not necessarily in itself be meaningful, but his juxtaposing these treatments in the same piece creates a striking internal opposition. Similarly, it would not be correct to assume that Vivaldi never assigns vordersatz, fortspinnung, and epilog functions to an episode[56] or that his ritornellos always have fortspinnung segments. What is noteworthy about Bach's procedure in the Sixth Brandenburg Concerto is that he categorically excludes fortspinnung segments from the ritornellos and includes them in a continually returning contrasted (i.e., "episode") section. It is not the presence in the Sixth Brandenburg Concerto of continually returning fortspinnung-type episodes or of ritornellos without fortspinnung segments that is necessarily significant.[57] The systematic opposition between these types of episodes and ritornellos generates the meaning.

In the context of this interpretation of relationships between structure and scoring, certain questions of organology in Bach research hold a greater interest than they might simply as factual issues. A great deal of research has been devoted especially to the continuo section of Bach's instrumentarium. For the Brandenburg Concertos this centers primarily on the violone parts. Scholars and performers generally consider Bach's violone to have been invariably a large double bass

---

[56] See, for example, the first episode in the third movement of Vivaldi's E-major violin concerto, Op. 3, no. 12 (RV 265; cf. Bach's arrangement of the piece for solo harpsichord, BWV 976).

[57] To object that fortspinnung is precluded in the ritornello by the formal constraints of canonic writing at the unison only invites a chicken-and-egg question. Bach may, of course, have chosen to compose the ritornello with canonic writing at the unison precisely because it precludes fortspinnung, and he may have chosen to include canonic writing at the seventh in the episode because this allows for fortspinnung.

sounding an octave below notated pitch. Laurence Dreyfus has argued recently, however, that Bach called for at least three different instruments by the name *violone* and that all three types show up in the Brandenburg Concertos.[58] Two of them are, to use the conventional terminology of organ pipes, in the 16' range, the one being a six-string type descending to a low D', and the other a four-string type with a low C'. Or to put it another way, the one is an oversized bass gamba and the other is an oversized cello. The third type of violone, apparently used by Bach only in his pre-Leipzig works, is a slightly oversized gamba in G' playing at pitch. Several details in the Sixth Brandenburg Concerto suggest the use of this 8' instrument. In one spot Bach briefly notates the violone part two octaves below the cello (see mm. 56–57 of the first movement), and in many other places he puts the two instruments an octave apart. In performance on a 16' violone this creates two-octave and even more unlikely and more unwieldy three-octave gaps between the bass instruments. Furthermore, the part descends at one point to a low B♭' (see m. 45 of the last movement), a pitch outside the range of the two larger violones but one easily negotiated on the smaller violone in G'.[59]

In light of the relationships between scoring and structure, it is also worth considering closely what type of gambas are called for in the upper parts of the Sixth Brandenburg Concerto. The two voices do not go below the A that lies a sixth above the lowest note on the cello. Although the parts are often played today on the seven-string bass gamba, they do not require the use of the lowest string on even the smaller, six-string bass gamba. It is possible, therefore, that the parts were designed for a still smaller gamba whose lowest string was

[58] Dreyfus, *Bach's Continuo Group*, pp. 136–66.

[59] See Richard Maunder, "The Violone in Bach's Brandenburg Concerti," *Galpin Society Journal* 31 (1978): 147, and Dreyfus, *Bach's Continuo Group*, p. 150. One might easily argue that when Bach composed or arranged the Sixth Brandenburg Concerto he was thinking in terms of a wide harpsichord range here, and he either forgot that the large violone cannot play the low B♭' or simply neglected to notate a separate reading an octave higher for it (ensembles today normally play the note up an octave). One could, however, counter that it was the other way around. In his exemplar Bach may have notated a separate reading an octave higher for the harpsichord. From the original separate parts to the Brandenburg Concertos, only those to the Fifth Concerto survive (Mus. ms. Bach St 130, Staatsbibliothek zu Berlin). Interestingly, the harpsichord part here avoids going below C. See m. 92 of the first movement, reading B' in the margrave's dedication score, but B both in St 130 and in the earliest version of the concerto, surviving in a copy made in the 1750s by Bach's son-in-law, Johann Christoph Altnickol (Mus. ms. Bach St 132).

tuned to G (i.e., the tenor gamba of the viol consort),[60] an instrument whose size is closer to the size of the viola, just as the size of the 8′ violone is close to the size of the cello. If so, this could mean that the concerto was set for six low string instruments arranged into two visually symmetrical groups on either side of the continuo harpsichord. On the one side would be the cello and the two violas (i.e., a large violin and two somewhat smaller violins, the large instrument being exactly an octave below the smaller instruments). And on the other side would be the 8′ violone and the two gambas (i.e., a large viol and two somewhat smaller viols, the large instrument being exactly an octave below the smaller instruments). It may be interesting also to note that for this visual contrast of the viola da gamba and violin families, neither family would be projected by its representative member: the violin itself and the bass viola da gamba would be (conspicuously) absent.

Experiencing a performance of this concerto, Prince Leopold of Köthen, Bach's employer at the time the Brandenburg Concertos were assembled, would surely have recognized immediately what was wrong with this picture. There were, after all, certain associations to account for the traditional treatment of string instruments in the early eighteenth century. And, as is not well known, not only Leopold but also his father, Emanuel Leberecht, devoted a great deal of energy to viola da gamba playing.[61] Whereas the viol had centu-

[60] Noting that normal gambas are often inaudible in larger concert halls, Harro Schmidt suggests that Bach's parts, including those in the Sixth Brandenburg Concerto, would be better served if played on the louder *Konzertgambe*, a (historical) gamba with a cello body (see "Die Viola da gamba der Violinfamilie: Ein vergessener Gambentyp des Barock," in *Alte Musik als ästhetische Gegenwart: Kongreßbericht Stuttgart 1985*, ed. Dietrich Berke and Dorothee Hanemann [Kassel: Bärenreiter, 1987], vol. 2, pp. 422–26). Schmidt does not go so far as to suggest using cellos. In any case, his observations would appear to be historically irrelevant to the Sixth Brandenburg Concerto, for we know that Bach's concertos were not performed in large concert halls and, furthermore, that the ranges of Bach's parts in the Sixth Brandenburg Concerto suggest the use of gambas that were not as large as cellos.

[61] See Philipp Spitta, *Johann Sebastian Bach* (Leipzig, 1873), vol. 1, p. 615; and Günther Hoppe, "Köthener politische, ökonomische und höfische Verhältnisse als Schaffensbedingungen Bachs (Teil 1)," *Cöthener Bach-Hefte* 4 (1986): 13–62, at p. 52, n. 55. In Köthen, Bach rescored the solo viola part from his Weimar cantata *Mein Herze schwimmt in Blut*, BWV 199, and the continuo cello part from Francesco Conti's *Languet anima mea* for gamba, presumably to accommodate Leopold's interests in the instrument; see Dreyfus, *Bach's Continuo Group*, p. 255, n. 58. Bach's scoring of the sonatas BWV 1014–19a, for violin and obbligato harpsichord with gamba doubling, possibly fits in here as well; on the authenticity of the scoring, from a manuscript copied in 1725, see

ries earlier been used as a more or less neutral consort instrument in Germany,[62] by the seventeenth and early eighteenth centuries it had taken on very special associations. In their use with the *stille Instrumenta*, the viols depict otherworldly comfort for mourners of death, as for example in Bach's early cantata *Gottes Zeit ist die allerbeste Zeit*, BWV 106, or in the "Köthener Trauermusik" (*Klagt, Kinder, Klagt es aller Welt*, BWV 244a); in another use with regal dotted figures, they stood for royalty (on account of their cultivation at the court of Louis XIV), as for example in Bach's triumphant aria "Es ist vollbracht" in the *St. John Passion*.[63] Not surprisingly, then, the gamba was a highly respected member of the musical establishment in the court at Köthen. Its player, Christian Ferdinand Abel, held the title of *Cammer Violagambist*, and compared to most of the other court musicians he received a substantial salary.[64]

The viola player, on the other hand, did not have such special privileges. His instrument had developed from the renaissance dance band of violins, and only gradually had the apparently crude instruments of the violin family been considered worthy to be admitted to aristocratic circles.[65] Even so, only the principal violin or violins of the orchestra ever achieved a relatively elevated social status within the musical hierarchy. References to violas (which were not played by soloists who specialized on this instrument) were unlikely even to show up in eighteenth-century court registers, and if they did at all they were much less likely to be associated specifically with a "Chamber Musician upon the Viola" than generally with a ripienist.

Schulze, *Studien zur Bach-Überlieferung*, p. 115. It should also be mentioned that the participation of the 8′ gamba-style violone would not preclude performance of the Sixth Brandenburg Concerto during Bach's tenure at Köthen; for complicated evidence suggesting that Bach must have written for this instrument at Köthen, see Marissen, "Relationships between Scoring and Structure," pp. 502–3.

[62] On the earlier history of the viol consort in Germany, see Ian Woodfield, *The Early History of the Viol* (Cambridge: Cambridge University Press, 1984), pp. 99–117 and 191–95.

[63] See Dreyfus, *Bach's Continuo Group*, pp. 166–69.

[64] See Hoppe, "Köthener politische, ökonomische und höfische Verhältnisse," p. 18. On the visual aspects of prestige construction with the baroque viola da gamba, see Richard Leppert, "Music, Representation, and Social Order in Early-Modern Europe," *Cultural Critique* 12 (1989): 25–55, at pp. 30–41.

[65] On the early history of the violin and its social status within the musical hierarchy, see David Boyden, *The History of Violin Playing, from Its Origins to 1761, and Its Relationship to the Violin and Violin Music* (London: Oxford University Press, 1965).

The viola player's relative social position and, correspondingly, his pay were low. His instrument carried no lofty associations. As a matter of fact, violas, if any associations were to be made for them at all, might, at least in some circles, still have been identified, even more readily than violins, with the world of beer-fiddling and other forms of lower-class life.[66] It is intriguing in this context to speculate that Bach's often-mentioned pleasure in playing the viola for chamber ensembles was related perhaps not merely (or even primarily?) to an interest in being "in the middle of the harmony" but also to a ready willingness to being placed in the socially least desirable position in the ensemble.[67]

APART FROM the fact that Prince Leopold of Köthen cultivated gamba and violin playing, there are other, even more interesting reasons to believe that he would have been struck by the social implications of the reversal of functions in the Sixth Brandenburg Concerto, where humble orchestral ripieno instruments play brilliant, solo chamber musicians' parts and privileged solo chamber instruments (perhaps favorites of Prince Leopold himself) play routine, ripieno musicians' parts.[68] Günther Hoppe, a curator at the museum of the city of Köthen, mentioned in a detailed study of the Köthen archives that Prince Leopold's assumption of the Köthen throne in 1716 was also celebrated in nearby Zerbst with a number of festivities,

[66] See, for example, the occasionally disparaging comments about viola players in Johann Joachim Quantz, *Versuch einer Anweisung die Flöte traversiere zu spielen* (Berlin, 1752), pp. 207–11. Note also that chamber-soloist violinists who may have also performed on the viola were identified with the term *violinist* in the court records, not with a more inclusive term like *string player* (i.e., the viola was then, as it is today, considered an instrument with a secondary status; see also n. 68).

[67] See Johann Nikolaus Forkel, *Über Johann Sebastian Bachs Leben, Kunst und Kunstwerk* (Leipzig, 1802), ed. Walther Vetter (Berlin: Henschel, 1966), p. 83; *The Bach Reader: A Life of Johann Sebastian Bach in Letters and Documents*, rev. ed., ed. Hans T. David and Arthur Mendel (New York: Norton, 1966), p. 334.

[68] The use of the word *instruments*, not *instrumentalists*, is intentional, because the viola, for example, would be considered a secondary instrument, regardless of whether Bach himself, privileged solo violinists of the court, or more lowly ripienists played it. Consider, for example, Quantz, *Versuch*, p. 249: "An honest musician must not be stubborn or be too enamored of his *rank* [*Rang*]. For example, an able violinist ought by no means to be ashamed if, in case of need, he must play the second violin, *or even* the viola" (emphases mine). (Quantz, *On Playing the Flute*, rev. ed., trans. and ed. Edward R. Reilly [New York: Schirmer, 1985], p. 273.) Questioning the status of the viola continues to this day: witness the huge repertory of "viola jokes."

several of them being somewhat unconventional for eighteenth-century Saxon princes.[69] These included an unusually extended series of musical performances as well as a learned oration attesting specifically to Leopold's interest in relationships between musical and political structures. This suggests that the attitude toward music making at Köthen was qualitatively different from some other courts, where the cultivation of music appears to have been solely a matter of entertainment.[70]

It is therefore not too difficult to imagine that Leopold tried occasionally to engage his Kapellmeister in discussions about correspondences between the given order in monarchical rule and the given order in music. Nor is it difficult to imagine that Leopold had a well above average knowledge of the influence of Vivaldi concerto form in Germany.[71] In the Sixth Brandenburg Concerto, even more so than in the other "Brandenburg" concertos, Bach appears to have been indulging both intellectual and musical interests—less, however, by reflecting the existing order than by challenging its assumptions.

THE FOURTH BRANDENBURG CONCERTO

One central question among the traditionally discussed problems surrounding the Fourth Brandenburg Concerto concerns its classification: is this a solo concerto for violin with ripieno strings and woodwinds, or is it a concerto grosso for a concertino of violin and woodwinds with ripieno strings?[72] In the preface to his edition of

---

[69] See n. 7 of the introduction.

[70] For example, the director of the *Königliche Capell- und Cammer-Musique* at Dresden was known from 1709 onward as the "Directeur des Plaisirs"; see Ortrun Landmann, "The Dresden Hofkapelle during the Lifetime of Johann Sebastian Bach," *Early Music* 17 (1989): 17–30, at p. 25.

[71] In this connection it is worth noting that in his letter of 28 October 1730 to Georg Erdmann in Danzig Bach states that "[in Cöthen] I had a gracious Prince, who both loved and *knew* music [Music so wohl liebenden als *kennenden* Fürsten]" (emphasis mine). See *Bach-Dokumente I: Schriftstücke von der Hand Johann Sebastian Bachs*, ed. Werner Neumann and Hans-Joachim Schulze (Kassel: Bärenreiter, 1963), pp. 67–68; and *Bach Reader*, p. 125.

[72] A longer version of this discussion has appeared as "Organological Questions and Their Significance in J. S. Bach's Fourth Brandenburg Concerto," *Journal of the American Musical Instrument Society* 17 (1991): 5–52.

the Brandenburg Concertos for the nineteenth-century publication of Bach's collected works, Wilhelm Rust, taking the solo-concerto view, refers to the autograph title and to the style of the work and claims that there is "no way one can speak of a triple concerto for violin with flutes."[73] Only a few years later, in his extended biography of Bach, Philipp Spitta, raising the concerto-grosso view, also refers to the autograph title and the style of the work and counters:

> [It] is a *Concerto grosso* in the manner of [Brandenburg Concerto] No. 2. . . . W. Rust, in the B.-G. edition, is wrong in calling it a violin concerto. The word *ripieni* in the title applies only to the violins, since there are no *flauti ripieni*. Besides this, the intention is clear from the work itself.[74]

The autograph title reads "Concerto 4to. à Violino Prencipale. due Fiauti d'Echo. due Violini, una Viola e Violone in Ripieno, Violoncello è / Continuo,"[75] and thus Spitta's observations turn out more accurately than Rust's to reflect the immediate text-critical facts. The force of Rust's conclusions depends somewhat on his having placed commas instead of periods before and after "due Fiauti d'Echo" in citing Bach's title.

Posing this sort of either/or question to the Fourth Brandenburg Concerto will hold certain practical consequences for us that would not necessarily have come up as an issue for Bach. For example, music publishers conventionally print groups of staves together, and their choices in formatting staves will reflect their classification, consciously or unconsciously considered, of the concerto.[76] Similarly, performers nowadays conventionally organize themselves on the concert stage into functional categories (e.g., soloists stand, while the other play-

[73] *Joh. Seb. Bachs Werke: Gesamtausgabe der Bachgesellschaft*, vol. 19: *Kammermusik, Dritter Band*, ed. Wilhelm Rust (Leipzig, 1869), p. vi.

[74] Spitta, *Johann Sebastian Bach: His Work and Influence on the Music of Germany*, trans. Clara Bell and J. A. Fuller-Maitland (London, 1889), vol. 2, pp. 133–34; and Spitta, *Johann Sebastian Bach*, vol. 1, p. 741.

[75] It is unclear whether Bach corrected the comma after "Ripieno" from a period.

[76] See Rust's edition, where the *Flauti I/II*, *Violino di ripieno I/II*, and *Violoncello/Violone* are grouped together by three separate brackets (i.e., solo-concerto formatting). Compare this with Besseler's edition for the *Neue Bach-Ausgabe*, where *Violino principale/Flauto dolce I/II* and *Violino in ripieno I/II/Viola in ripieno / Violoncello/Violone/Continuo* are grouped together by two separate brackets (i.e., triple-concerto formatting).

ers sit), and their setups will betray their view of the piece.[77] But taking into account Bach's notation of the staves in the margrave of Brandenburg's score (which has no bracketing of subgroups) and carefully considering what the setup procedures for Bach's own performances of the piece could have been (did Bach group his instrumentalists functionally?), we might find the either/or question to have a false urgency. The very ambiguity of classification for the Fourth Brandenburg Concerto might instead, as I will argue, be interpreted as an interesting aspect of the meaning of the piece.

Even from a superficial glance at the score it is clear that Bach's violino prencipale part commands, by its overt virtuosity, a great deal of attention within the ensemble. It is also clear that the fiauti d'echo parts command, by their thematic prominence, more attention than the ripieno string parts. This is, of course, why it was possible in the first place to sustain extended discussion of whether this is a solo or triple concerto. But Bach may in fact be moving beyond the two-way (concertino/tutti) textural contrast of the traditional baroque concerto and making it three-way: one soloist versus two other soloists, and these together against the ensemble. Moreover, the oppositions may be seen to involve not only musical ones between full and reduced textures, between string and woodwind instrumental timbres, and so on but also deeper, social oppositions between first-rank and second-rank instruments within the ensemble.

IN ORDER TO pursue the social aspects of this interpretation, we need to be certain about what instruments Bach called for with his designation "Fiauti d'Echo." Although this issue has long been controversial among musicologists, instrument makers, and players, much of the research on the question, both published and unpublished, has been either unrigorous or too limited in scope. All sorts of instruments, in various sizes and tunings, have been suggested (seeking immediately practical solutions for performances, however, ensembles today generally capitulate toward either the transverse flute or the alto recorder in f'). Elsewhere, I have explored the relevant aspects in Bach's notational habits, instrumental writing, and terminology and concluded that Bach must have designed the

[77] I have witnessed several performances of the Fourth Brandenburg Concerto with the woodwind players standing next to the solo violinist and several other performances with them sitting next to the ripieno strings.

Fourth Brandenburg Concerto for two standard alto recorders (i.e., instruments upon which placing all fingers down produces the note f').[78]

As WITH the previous discussions, I will consider formal aspects before interpreting Bach's scoring socially in terms of court-ensemble figuration.

In all three movements of the Fourth Brandenburg Concerto, Bach extends the instrumental contrasts beyond typical ones between tutti and solo to include exploration of less conventional oppositions between the instruments that do not belong to the ripieno-strings section of the ensemble. By various means, Bach appears to bring up the roles for the recorders—having them act as prominent members of both concertino and ripieno groups—and to draw back the soloistic centrality of the violin.

Unconventional relationships between soloists are most apparent in the peculiar stylistic environment of Bach's slow movement. Bach structures the rhythm of the Andante as in a French sarabande: the music flows in a slow, triple meter with accents on the second beats of the measures and with hemiolas at the cadences. And at the same time he structures the thematic material as in a Vivaldian concerto movement: mm. 1–18 have the characteristic features of a tonally closed ritornello with vordersatz, fortspinnung, and epilog segments (points of division occuring at mm. 9, 13, and 16); and subsections of this opening period come back throughout the movement. But the textural contrasts conform to neither the conventions of the orchestral sarabande nor those of the concerto. In Vivaldian concertos the concertino episodes are typically framed, of course, by orchestral ritornellos. And in French orchestral dance music the trio episodes are typically scored for two recorders and viola.[79] In Bach's Andante, however, trio concertino textures appear in various guises: first, as echoes within ritornello segments (see mm. 3–5, 7–9, 10–11, 12–13, and their transpositions); second, as echoes within orchestrally scored

[78] See Marissen, "Organological Questions and Their Significance," pp. 6–27, 34–42. A more general survey of some of these issues is found in Marissen, "Bach-Repertoire für Flötisten," *Tibia* 12 (1987): pp. 537–40.

[79] Or two oboes and bassoon, or three solo string instruments. See James R. Anthony, *French Baroque Music from Beaujoyeulx to Rameau*, rev. ed. (New York: Norton, 1978), p. 106.

episodes (see mm. 20–21 and 23–24 and their transpositions—the example of mm. 23–24, however, is not a note-for-note echo); third, as interludes within orchestrally scored episodes (see the trio passages of mm. 18–19 and its transposition, as well as solo-recorder passages in mm. 29–30, 31–32, and 68–69); and fourth, even as a substitute for the tutti within a ritornello statement (see the ritornello of mm. 61–67, where the fortspinnung segment appears in trio texture before the epilog segment appears more properly in tutti texture). The scoring of these unconventional tutti-solo contrasts is for a concertino trio of two recorders and the principal violin (not viola) against the ensemble.

Bach assigns a strikingly secondary role to the solo violin throughout this movement. In the outer sections of the movement's quasi-symmetrical structure of five blocks,[80] the three soloists for the most part double the ripieno violins in the tutti statements, whereas in the concertino-textured echoes or interludes the recorders assume the main voice and the solo violin takes on an accompanying *Bassätchen* function.

It is perhaps in this connection that the significance of Bach's title for the Fourth Brandenburg Concerto emerges. His heading reads: "Concerto 4to. à Violino Prencipale. due Fiauti d'Echo. due Violini, una Viola è Violone in Ripieno, Violoncello è Continuo." This use of the term *echo* following an instrumental designation is unique in Bach. And this use of the term *prencipale* attached to the violin, though common in Italian concertos of the period, is nearly unique for Bach. The only other place he employs it is in the solo violin part to the revised versions of the Fifth Brandenburg Concerto.[81] Consider, then, Bach's employment of the linguistic parallelism "Violino *Prencipale*"— "Fiauti *d'Echo*." The former predicate is clearly employed to designate not a special kind of violin but rather the role of the violin in this

[80] That is, compare mm. 1–18 with 55–71 and mm. 18–28 with 45–55.

[81] The second version is transmitted in the set of autograph parts, Mus. ms. Bach St 130 (Staatsbibliothek zu Berlin), and the nearly identical third version is transmitted in the margrave of Brandenburg's dedication score (Berlin, Am.B.78). The markedly different earliest version is transmitted in the set of parts Mus. ms. Bach St 132. These parts were copied by Bach's son-in-law, Johann Christoph Altnickol, who labels the part "Violino concertato." It is also worth pointing out that the wrapper to the set of Köthen parts (St 130) refers to "Violino Obligato" (see Dürr, "Zur Entstehungsgeschichte des 5. Brandenburgischen Konzerts," *Bach-Jahrbuch* 61 [1975]: 63–69).

piece. Similarly, the latter predicate would designate not (necessarily) a special kind of fiauto but perhaps rather the function of the instrument (i.e., it would refer to "recorders of the echo," not instruments called "echo-recorders").

Bach's "d'Echo" may well refer to the function of the recorders, but perhaps not merely to the obvious *piano* effects in the Andante.[82] The word *echo* implies a secondary, relatively powerless function. For example, the Echo of ancient mythology could speak using only the words, or consecutive syllables, she had just heard. She could, however, intend them in a different sense from the original speaker.[83] The term *prencipale*, on the other hand, is very commonly attached to *violino* in Italian concertos, where it accurately describes the principal (primary, or relatively powerful) function of the solo violin part. Perhaps Bach's terms are best interpreted ironically, for the parallelism of his designations suggests a secondary role for the recorders and a primary role for the violin. But, obviously, in the slow movement at

---

[82] I am aware of one example outside Bach in which "Flauto Eco" also appears to refer to the standard recorder in f'. The F-major aria "Canoro rosignuolo" in *Il Fiore delle eroine* by Giovanni Bononcini (performed in 1704, in Vienna) is scored with "2 Flauti" and "2 *Flauti Eco*." Because the range for both pairs of instruments is exactly the same and because the "Eco" pair merely imitates the ends of the normal recorders' phrases, "Eco" would seem to refer merely to the function of the second pair of recorders (which apparently were also standard f' recorders and not some special type of instrument). It is worth noting that Bononcini also uses the term *echo* in the same way for the aria "Lieti geplausi" in *Euleo festeggianti nel ritorno d'Allessandro Magno dall'Indie* (performed in 1699, in Vienna). Here "2 *Trombe Ecco*" imitate solo trumpet and tenor. It seems especially unlikely that Bononcini's "Trombe Ecco" were some sort of mechanically altered instrument (since any kind of trumpet can play loudly and softly, Bononcini's "Ecco" would most logically have functional, not organological, significance). These examples are discussed in Ernst Kubitschek, "Block- und Querflöte im Umkreis von J. J. Fux: Versuch einer Übersicht," in *Johann Joseph Fux und die barocke Bläsertradition: Kongreßbericht Graz 1985*, ed. Bernhard Habla (Tutzing: Schneider, 1987), pp. 99–119, at pp. 103–4.

[83] Thus, for example, in the echo aria "Treues Echo dieser Orten" from Bach's cantata "Hercules auf dem Scheidewege" (*Laßt uns sorgen, laßt uns wachen*), BWV 213, Echo will iterate a final, tonally closing "ja" or "nein" not spoken immediately before that by Hercules. That is, Hercules' interrogative "ja" becomes Echo's indicative "ja." (See also the adaptation of this aria as "Flößt, mein Heiland, flößt dein Namen" in the fourth part of the Christmas Oratorio, BWV 248.) One of the most striking examples in baroque music of this sort of echo procedure involving changes in meaning occurs in the motet "Audio, coelum" from Claudio Monteverdi's *Vespro della Beata Vergine* (Venice, 1610), where "gaudio" turns into Eco's "Audio!" and "benedicam" becomes "Dicam!"

least, the actual functions are reversed: the recorders are in fact primary, and the solo violin is secondary.[84]

An easily overlooked notational peculiarity of Bach's dedication copy for the margrave of Brandenburg strengthens this interpretation. The top line of the score might strike us as an obvious place for a violino prencipale line, but the standard ordering for orchestral scores in Germany during Bach's lifetime was: trumpet–timpani–horn–flute/recorder–oboe–(solo and ripieno) violins–viola–continuo.[85] Thus in the few extant original scores of Bach's violin concertos including woodwind parts in the orchestra, the solo violin appears in the middle of the score, not the top (as, for example, in the D-major Sinfonia, BWV 1045, surviving only as a fragment,[86] or the third movement of the First Brandenburg Concerto). In arias with obbligatos for woodwind and string instruments but no ripieno string section, Bach likewise normally notates the woodwinds above the obbligato strings.[87] For the Andante in the Fourth Brandenburg Concerto, it would have been visually appealing and, certainly on the

[84] A similar reversal in significance and function can be seen in the echo aria from the Christmas Oratorio (see n. 83). We know from recent studies of the theological traditions behind seventeenth and eighteenth-century German poetry that the (ostensibly weak) echo answering the soprano's prayers has to be understood to be the voice of (the all-powerful) Christ. See Ernst Koch, "Tröstendes Echo: Zur theologischen Deutung der Echo-Arie im IV. Teil des Weihnachts-Oratoriums von Johann Sebastian Bach," *Bach-Jahrbuch* 75 (1989): 203–11.

[85] See Klaus Haller, *Partituranordnung und musikalischer Satz* (Tutzing: Schneider, 1970), pp. 223–32.

[86] Mus. ms. Bach P 614, Staatsbibliothek zu Berlin. There are no surviving autograph scores to Bach vocal works in which the orchestral staves include one or more staves for woodwind as well as a solo violin part with its own separate staff throughout the score. (The complicated relationship, however, between the peculiar notations of the concertato violin parts in the cantatas *Angenehmes Wiederau, freue dich in deinen Auen!* BWV 30a [Mus. ms. Bach P 43], and *Freue dich, erlöste Schar*, BWV 30 [Mus. ms. Bach P 44], is discussed in Prinz, "Studien zum Instrumentarium," pp. 29–30.)

[87] Prinz, "Studien zum Instrumentarium," p. 32; at pp. 32–33 Prinz also points out curious exceptions to this in the cantatas *Brich dem Hungrigen dein Brot*, BWV 39, and *Gott ist unsre Zuversicht*, BWV 197. In the former, the aria "Seinem Schöpfer noch auf Erden"—scored for oboe, violin, alto, and continuo—is notated with the violin above the oboe (although Bach's heading correctly reads "Aria 1 Hautb è 1 Violino"). In the latter, Bach notates the aria "Vergnügen und Lust"—scored for violin, two oboes, soprano, and continuo—with the violin above the oboes (he arranged this from the aria "Ich lasse dich nicht" in his cantata *Ehre sei Gott in der Höhe*, BWV 197a, where the scoring was for oboe, bass, and continuo—that is, transposing these parts for the BWV 197 arrangement, Bach assigned the original obbligato for oboe to violin and enriched the aria with chordal filler played by a pair of oboes).

face of it, musically more logical to have conformed to the conventions of eighteenth-century German score arrangement (i.e., by placing the two recorders above the solo violin). To do so would have put the bass line of the concertino sections properly beneath the two soprano lines. Interestingly, however, Bach's notation of the violin part at the top of the score might be interpreted to call all the greater attention to the secondary character of the solo violin part within the concertino.[88]

The discrepancies of functions for the concertino instruments in the Andante can be explored a bit further by considering their relationship to another curious stylistic feature of the movement. Although it was already mentioned that the ritornello sections of the movement bring together rhythmic properties of French orchestral sarabandes and thematic properties of Vivaldian concertos, it is also worth considering the significance of French and Italian stylistic traits in the episodes. In mm. 29, 31, and 68–69, the French sarabande rhythm and texture is broken by the insertion of short, Italianate improvisatory passages. Interestingly, these cadenzas are scored for the first recorder, something that may be considered doubly inappropriate. This isolates the first recorder from its stylistically inseparable partner, the second recorder. And, in a second way of making essentially the same observation, so long as there are going to be Italianate improvisatory passages in this sarabande, it would seem that the solo violin would have been the more obviously appropriate vehicle for them (i.e., since the violin is the more readily separable solo instrument within the concertino). Furthermore, although it is well known that the origins of the baroque violin are Italian, it may not be so well known that the origins of the baroque recorder are French. This only heightens a general sense of the violin's being snubbed in this slow movement: the French duet-instrument takes on a stylistic prerogative of the Italian solo instrument.[89]

---

[88] Haller, *Partituranordnung*, p. 152, suggests that Bach notated the violin part at the top of the score to call attention to the fact that this is essentially a solo violin concerto, not a triple concerto, although the two woodwind instruments, as he puts it, "certainly do occasionally 'intrude' upon the solo violin."

[89] On the French origins of the baroque recorder, see, for example, Edgar Hunt, *The Recorder and Its Music*, rev. ed. (London: Eulenburg, 1977), chap. 3. This described polarity between the soloists would of course be lost in Bach's substituting the solo violin with the obbligato harpsichord for the F-major version of the concerto (BWV 1057). There (partly because of this lost polarity?) Bach has the harpsichord alone take

Differing degrees of tension between the recorders and violin are also maintained in the two fast movements from this concerto. Consider first the extraordinarily long ritornello of the opening Allegro (mm. 1–83). Measures 1–13 are scored with the two recorders at the center of attention, while the rest of the orchestra, including the solo violin, assumes a secondary, written-out basso continuo function. Bach organizes the rhythm of this material as in a 3/8 minuet, grouped in two-measure units.[90] In fact, the length of this section roughly corresponds to the length necessary for the standard Z formation of dance steps in the baroque minuet.[91] This court dance was cultivated as a strict and formal affair in which the social hierarchy was rigidly respected: the most prominent couple was the first to execute the elegant dance steps, as the others looked on. Bach's scoring of the excerpt can be viewed to provide an instrumental allusion to this sort of social situation. The strings look on with first-beat accompanimental chords, while the pair of recorders alone outlines the *pas de minuet à deux mouvements* dance pattern.[92] This bit of material returns in mm.

---

over all the concertino-textured material in the slow movement. I would not argue, incidentally, that the trumpet is being snubbed by its exclusion from the slow movement to the Second Brandenburg Concerto. The (conventional) absence of brass in slow movements to concertos allows the players much-needed rest, and this practice in fact reinforces the prominence of brass instruments by setting starkly in relief the return of their participation for the fast movements. If, however, a standard, primary solo instrument does participate in a strikingly secondary way throughout a movement (something I have not encountered outside Bach), it would warrant being described as having been snubbed.

[90] Among Bach's instrumental movements expressly designated by him as a minuet, the only one with a 3/8 time signature is found in the Suite in A minor, BWV 818a, a movement also featuring arpeggiated sixteenth-note motion in the head of its opening theme. Bach's pre-1724 arias in minuet style are notated in 3/4, and from 1724 on they are notated in 3/8, perhaps owing to Vivaldi's influence. See Doris Finke-Hecklinger, *Tanzcharaktere in Johann Sebastian Bachs Vokalmusik* (Trossingen: Hohner, 1970), p. 46.

[91] The basic step pattern of the minuet consists of four steps taken to six beats (described in n. 92). Thus the basic unit is two measures (in 3/4 or 3/8), not one or four, and there is not necessarily a strong accent on the second downbeat. Since the letter-Z floor design ordinarily took six step patterns to execute, the ideal musical strain would be twelve bars long (just as many of Jean-Baptiste Lully's minuets for Louis XIV's court are twelve bars long; many composers more often wrote in eight-measure or sixteen-measure strains). See Little, "Minuet," pp. 353–58.

[92] Bach's beat pattern conforms remarkably closely to the demands of the popular pattern *pas de minuet à deux mouvements*, in which the *demi-coupé* (bend and rise) occurs twice and is followed twice by the *pas marché* (step on the ball of the foot). The *élevé* (rise) of the first *demi-coupé* is on the right foot and the second is on the left, occurring

23–35 in the dominant and in mm. 57–69 in the tonic, interspersed by blocks of sequential material and concluded by a hemiola block that brings the macro-block of mm. 1–83 to a formal division marked by tonal closure. In other words, it turns out that the opening minuet gesture can be reinterpreted as a vordersatz segment returning within a Vivaldian orchestral ritornello otherwise subdivided by a number of sequential fortspinnung segments and a closing hemiola epilog (with the fortspinnung segments starting in mm. 13, 35, 43, 47, and 69, and the epilog in m. 79).

After such an unusually extended ritornello with its own internal returns of the vordersatz segment and with some of its own internal textural contrasts, Bach's relatively modest entry in m. 83 for the solo violin with the sole accompaniment of pedal-point continuo seems by comparison, strangely, to be a bit of a disappointment. With lackluster, chordal thematic lines over pedal points in two-measure groupings, the violin wends its way from mm. 83 and 105 for the duration of half-Z formations. It also sequences from mm. 91 and 113 for the duration of a full-Z formation, three times interrupted by the tutti quotations of the head of the opening vordersatz segment (see mm. 89, 103, and 111). A thematically more deliberate sense of movement picks up in m. 125 with episodic sequential material derived from the ritornello (see mm. 35–43). In other words, the violin, when it has its own thematic material, proceeds in a (comparatively speaking) static manner. It seems to rely on the invocation of material derived from the ritornello (dominated by the recorders) to get things moving more purposively. And this ritornello-derived material of mm. 125 and following brings a modulation not to the dominant (the direction the violin had been heading, conforming to stylistic conventions for the first return of the opening ritornello in a baroque concerto move-

---

on beats one and three of the first measure. The first *plié* (bend) is on the upbeat to the measure and the second is on beat two. The first *pas marché* is on the right foot and the second is on the left, occurring on beats one and two of the second measure. Bach's stylized Allegro minuet strain is notated in 3/8, like Italian-baroque minuets, but the beat patterns adhere closely to the slower 3/4 French minuet. That is, Italian minuets have longer phrases than the French (usually eight bars, rather than two or four), and they make more use of sequencing to sustain a clear sense of direction. On the characteristics of the French and Italian minuet, see Little, "Minuet," pp. 353–56. Considering the opening gestures of the first two movements of the Fourth Brandenburg Concerto as related to the minuet and sarabande, we might also view Bach switching around here the sarabande-to-minuet ordering of the baroque dance suite.

ment), but to the relative minor. Interestingly, in this procedure, it is the recorders who have again assumed the principal voice.

Only the recorders end up generating a genuine solo theme within this Allegro (see mm. 157–85). This appears to set off a series of stylistically unconventional reactions in the solo violin part. The subsequent vordersatz segment of supertonic ritornello (mm. 185 and following) becomes nearly overwhelmed by a burst of running thirty-second-note histrionics from the solo violin. From the point of view of convention, this is, of course, strongly inappropriate. The place in concertos for such overt virtuosity is in solo episodes, not orchestral ritornellos. Furthermore, its inappropriateness is especially marked in this case, because, as was noted before, the vordersatz segment of the ritornello can be viewed as alluding to the standard formation of dance steps in the baroque minuet, a dignified and elegant court dance in which such outbursts would have been severely frowned upon. Thus, to invoke the ready notion of "decorated ritornello" in describing this section would be, in my view, to fail to have captured the exceptional sense of the passage. (It would not be essentially different, for example, from describing the extraordinary moment effected by the initial bass entry of the augmentation canon on the chorale melody *Dies sind die heilgen zehn Gebot* in Bach's much-discussed cantata *Du sollt Gott, deinen Herren, lieben*, BWV 77, as a "diatonic tetrachord.")

A stylistically more restrained sort of virtuosity pervades the subdominant ritornello in mm. 209 and following. Here the violin shows up the two recorders from a different angle. Instead of drawing attention to itself by means of frenzied virtuosic material distinct from the recorders' more staid material (as it did up to this point in the movement), the violin now appears intent to assert its superiority by taking on the recorders' parallel-thirds theme by itself (i.e., through double-stopping). Furthermore, the violin performs the theme without the necessity for breathing: the characteristic rests in the recorder parts are replaced by the tied-over parallel sixths in the solo violin part (mm. 217–20).[93] This, however, may obfuscate slightly the original clarity of the first step of each group of *pas marché*

---

[93] This point was made by Reinhard Goebel, "J. S. Bach: Die Brandenburgischen Konzerte," *Concerto*, no. 8 (1987): 16–18, at p. 18; see also no. 9 (1987): 10–11. As Goebel puts it of the violin, "All right then, flutes, step aside—I'll do it better!"

steps in the minuet rhythm,[94] and so, perhaps partly for this reason, the recorders join the continuo here to mark the downbeat of the second measures for each of the two-measure dance units.

A secondary role for the solo violin within a concertino of three treble instruments can also be traced in the third movement of the concerto. For several of the episodes in this concerto-style fugue (Bach structures the ritornello as a fugal exposition), the violin acts as a sort of rhythmic continuo while the recorders assume the principal contrapuntal voices (see mm. 41–63 and 179–203). In its one venture into overt virtuosity (mm. 87–127) the violin degenerates into technical puffery that is at the same time more extreme and more pointless than it was in the opening Allegro. Impervious to the tutti instruments in the measures following 95 and 105, the violin forges ahead, the eventual close appearing designed to be anticlimactic. (In the case of mm. 105 and following, there are ritornello fragments in the ripieno—uncharacteristically, not marked *piano*—which perhaps are intended, as it were, to remind the wayward soloist of the truth from which it is deviating.[95]) The rhythmic drive slows from sixteenths to eighths in m. 120, which, instead of cadencing on the goal of E minor, arrives on the dominant of its subdominant. Moreover, when the initially undermined arrival does in fact occur at m. 127, the violin turns out tonally to be exactly where it had started, in E minor. (The beginning of the episode, m. 87, was marked by an E-minor cadence of the fugal tutti.) This assessment of the vanity of the violin's virtuosity is further heightened by observing that not only all the other episodes in this movement but also all the internal ritornellos modulate.

IT SEEMS, then, that the traditional dilemma concerning whether the Fourth Brandenburg Concerto is a solo concerto for violin with ripieno recorders and strings or a triple concerto for violin, two recorders, and ripieno strings could be abandoned for a new, third way of looking at the work. The answer to the either/or classification ques-

---

[94] See the definitions in n. 92.

[95] It is intriguing to notice that histrionics are rare in Bach's concertos and that when they do occur, they are often accompanied by ritornello fragments in the orchestra (see, e.g., mm. 105–16 of the third movement from the A-minor violin concerto, BWV 1041).

tion could be "both and neither." On closer consideration of Bach's treatment of the instruments, the piece would appear essentially to be a triple concerto with tension-filled surface leanings toward the solo concerto. The scoring is for two recorders (technically unimposing but often thematically central), a solo violin (technically ostentatious but often thematically less central), and ripieno strings.

This general elevating of the recorder at the more than occasional expense of the violin probably ought not to be viewed merely as a creative or clever deviation from conventions of eighteenth-century instrumental treatment. It is worth considering the significance of the fact that at the time the Brandenburg Concertos were compiled, the recorder and the violin were virtually at opposite ends of the musical hierarchy. In the early eighteenth century, the first (i.e., solo) violin position was the most prestigious in the court orchestra, next to that of the conductor.[96] The recorder, on the other hand, was at this time a secondary orchestral instrument of the oboist and a chamber instrument of the (mostly middle-class) amateur (hence the large repertory of technically and musically unassuming recorder sonatas published in the early eighteenth century). It had become extremely rare for court payroll records to list musicians specifically as recorder players. In orchestral music the recorder was used mainly as a special-effects instrument. It was associated, for example, with pastoral scenes or with death, and composers most typically called for pairs of f' instruments. The parts were played either by court oboists (in the event that the court had titled oboists), who it was tacitly assumed were able to play the recorder, or, perhaps even more commonly, by members from the municipal music guilds who were specially hired for the occasions. Even in the *Stadtpfeiferei* (what these municipal guilds were called in Germany) the recorder was only a secondary instrument and therefore was typically not mentioned or included in the examination requirements.[97] In short, the recorder then had, as it still has today, a relatively low status in the musical hierarchy.

[96] On the position of the solo violin, see p. 34 here.

[97] See Dietz Degen, *Zur Geschichte der Blockflöte in den germanischen Ländern* (Kassel: Bärenreiter, 1936), p. 91. On the history of the *Stadtpfeiferei* in Germany, see Martin Wolschke, *Von der Stadtpfeiferei zur Lehrlingskapelle und Sinfonieorchester* (Regensburg: Bosse, 1981). On the later situation in Köthen, see Herbert Zimpel, "In der Köthener Stadtpfeiferakte geblättert," *Cöthener Bach-Hefte* 3 (1985): 65–71.

Bach's subtle and peculiar deflating of the high-ranking violin and distinguishing of the low-ranking recorders within manipulations of minuet, sarabande, concerto, and fugal structures in the Fourth Brandenburg Concerto, seen, then, in this light as a social allegory of sorts,[98] can gain a greater significance than one of artistic novelty. In the present interpretation, Bach appears to view commonly held—though tacit—social assumptions as unwarranted value judgments (are violins inherently "better" than recorders?). Moreover, stretching this interpretive idea to its broadest historically tenable limits, I would argue that he may well have considered such uncritical views to be dissonant with his Lutheran beliefs:[99] according to the Reformation doctrine of the priesthood of all believers, in God's eyes individuals or classes are not better than others, regardless of their earthly status. More subtly, the relationships set up by the composer-"creator" between scoring and structure in the Fourth Brandenburg Concerto might also be seen to allegorize, even more clearly than the other concertos of the margrave's set, the relationships between the Creator's "alien" and "proper work." According to Luther, God's real (proper) work involves raising people up to salvation from sin, a process far from immediately apparent in daily life on this dreary earth. This proper work is much more readily perceived as alien, in that it involves God's striking people down in realization of their sin, that is, an action by which they will be raised up to salvation.[100] In elevating

---

[98] For a similar social interpretation involving recorder and violin, see Marissen, "A Trio in C Major for Recorder, Violin, and Continuo by J. S. Bach?" *Early Music* 13 (1985): 384–90, and "A Critical Reappraisal of J. S. Bach's A-Major Flute Sonata," *Journal of Musicology* 6 (1988): 367–86.

[99] Following the discovery of Bach's heavily annotated personal Bible, the sincerity of his religious beliefs can no longer be readily dismissed; see Howard H. Cox, ed., *The Calov Bible of J. S. Bach* (Ann Arbor: UMI Research Press, 1985). For a systematic survey of Lutheran theology, see Paul Althaus, *The Theology of Martin Luther*, trans. Robert C. Schultz (Philadelphia: Fortress Press, 1966). The relevance of theological matters and the Calov Bible for social interpretation of Bach's music will be discussed at greater length in part 3.

[100] See one of Bach's interesting treatments of this idea in the cantata, *Wer sich selbst erhöhet, der soll erniedriget werden*, BWV 47, in particular the soprano aria, within whose B section virtuosic double-stop violin playing accompanies the text on God's association of pride with the devil, as contrasted to the association of meekness with Christ in the A section. Another interesting example associating violin histrionics with hell, vanity, and the like is the alto aria in the cantata *Wer mich liebet, der wird mein Wort halten*, BWV 74.

the lowly fiauti d'echo (to frequent positions of primary status within both the concertino and the ripieno) and by stealthily bringing down somewhat the supereminent violino prencipale (at best, to *primus inter pares* status), Bach may be considered to have created in the Fourth Brandenburg Concerto an unparalleled structure representing musically the breach between appearance and essence familiar from everyday social and religious experience.

CHAPTER TWO

The Six Concertos
as a Set

THE currently favored view in scholarly writing on the Brandenburg Concertos is that they represent less a meaningful set
than a collection of individual, unrelated works in the genre.[1] On the
face of it, the reasons for this view would appear uncontroversial.
Each of the concertos in the collection calls for a different scoring,
and, equally significant, the tonal structure (F–F–G–G–D–B♭) conforms to no clearly recognizable scheme. Furthermore, the concertos
share neither the same number of movements nor the same stylistic
orientations. We might conclude from this, as well as from the fact
that secondary copies of earlier versions to some of the concertos survive, that the concertos were probably composed over an extended
period of time.

For most students of Bach's music who assume this position the
problem is merely a matter of straightforward description, a catalog of
the master's works. That is, the conclusion that the Brandenburg
Concertos probably constitute an arbitrary set has no significance be-

[1] A slightly different version of this discussion has appeared as "J. S. Bach's Bran-
denburg Concertos as a Meaningful Set," *Musical Quarterly* 77 (1993): 193–235. See
Walter Emery's comments regarding the collection in Christoph Wolff, *The New Grove
Bach Family* (New York: Norton, 1983), p. 155; Pippa Drummond, *The German Concerto:
Five Eighteenth-Century Studies* (Oxford: Clarendon Press, 1980), p. 27; Martin Geck,
"Gattungstraditionen und Altersschichten in den Brandenburgischen Konzerten," *Die
Musikforschung* 23 (1970): 139–52; Johannes Krey, "Zur Entstehungsgeschichte des erst-
en Brandenburgischen Konzerts," in *Festschrift Heinrich Besseler zum sechzigsten Geburtstag*,
ed. Institut für Musikwissenschaft der Karl-Marx-Universität (Leipzig: VEB Deutscher
Verlag für Musik, 1961), pp. 337–42, at p. 337; and Heinrich Besseler, ed., *Johann
Sebastian Bach, Neue Ausgabe sämtlicher Werke* (*Neue Bach Ausgabe*, hereafter *NBA*, followed by vol. and part nos.), vol. 7, part 2: *Sechs Brandenburgische Konzerte*, Kritischer
Bericht (Kassel: Bärenreiter, 1956), pp. 22–23. To avoid a specific misunderstanding, I
am intentionally not employing the word *cycle*. In current musicological writing on
various composers, this word commonly refers to a collection whose members are so
intimately related to each other that they would not successfully stand on their own as
discrete works; that is, the collection is the "work." I would not argue that the Brandenburg Concertos ought to be seen as a cycle in this sense.

yond its implications for a chronology of Bach's works. In Martin Geck's closer and more sophisticated study of the concertos, however, the claims are stronger and more far-reaching.[2] Geck suggests that we will understand the Brandenburg Concertos only if we do not consider them as a whole. We will not be taking the individuality of the pieces seriously if we view them as contrasting members within a collection. Bach's putting together the six pieces will be recognized as more or less arbitrary once we realize that the pieces probably come from different periods in his career and therefore would necessarily reflect different compositional thinking. Seen in this light, performances of the entire collection, especially those moving from left to right (i.e., consecutively from 1 to 6), may be considered not only historically improbable (unauthentic: contrary to "the way it was"[3]) but also stylistically illegitimate (unauthentic in the deep sense: contrary to "the way it 'is' "[4]).

Goethe, commenting on Handel's *Messiah*, addresses the idea that compilations necessarily lack any sense of meaningful whole when composers assemble pieces originating from different periods in their careers. Goethe's friend Carl Friedrich Zelter, then the director of the Berlin Singakademie, suggested that *Messiah* was probably not conceived as a whole, but was more or less an arbitrary compilation of individual sections. To this observation Goethe, a great lover of the work, replied, "I am not disinclined to accept the idea that it is a collection, a compilation from a rich source of supply: since fundamentally it does not matter in the least whether the unity is formed at the beginning or the end."[5]

We may reasonably assume that Bach did assemble the six Brandenburg Concertos from a somewhat larger supply of pieces. The autograph scores of sinfonias from his Leipzig church cantatas, for

[2] Geck, "Gattungstraditionen und Altersschichten."

[3] That is, ensembles in the early eighteenth century probably would not have performed the Brandenburg Concertos in consecutive order; nor, for that matter, would they have performed the entire collection in one sitting.

[4] The listener would focus on the contrasting treatment of surface aspects (e.g., virtuosity) throughout the collection and therefore would inevitably be too preoccupied to experience the deeper, structural individuality of the works presupposed by their varying compositional origins.

[5] Letter of 28 April 1824 to Zelter, quoted in this translation in the pocket score: Georg Friedrich Händel, *The Messiah*, ed. John Tobin (Leipzig: VEB Deutscher Verlag für Musik, 1968), p. x.

example, are typically neat copies, whereas the subsequent vocal movements look rather messy.[6] Presumably some of these sinfonias—especially those from Bach's first few, extremely hectic years in Leipzig—were copied from now lost Köthen or Weimar concertos, and some of them, as is well known, were copied from concertos that have survived (several cantatas, as mentioned earlier, take their sinfonias from movements that also show up, in slightly different form, in the Brandenburg Concertos[7]). Also, Bach appears to have arranged nearly all his solo and multiple harpsichord concertos in Leipzig from earlier scorings for strings and woodwinds, and some of these were presumably conceived in Weimar and Köthen. In assembling six of his concertos for the margrave of Brandenburg, Bach made certain choices, and these choices may have resulted in not an arbitrary but a meaningful set.[8]

The question of what constitutes a meaningful set may be illuminated by considering counterexamples from other well-known instrumental collections of Bach's. (It is well beyond the scope of this book, however, to provide the details for why scholars consider these collections to be meaningful sets.) Part 3 of the *Clavier-Übung* (BWV 552, 669–89, and 802–5) is generally acknowledged to be a meaningful set, though it contains works of very widely differing styles and genres.[9] Part 1 of the *Well-Tempered Clavier* (BWV 846–69) also contains works of differing styles, and, interestingly, it is documented that Bach more

[6] For details on this, see Robert L. Marshall, *The Compositional Process of J. S. Bach* (Princeton: Princeton University Press, 1972).

[7] See n. 11 of the introduction.

[8] We do not know how Bach himself kept the six Brandenburg Concertos in his personal library. There is no evidence to confirm or contradict his having preserved them as a set: contrary to the information given or implied in Besseler, *NBA* 7.2, Kritischer Bericht, all secondary copies of the Brandenburg Concertos stem either from the margrave's score or from sets of performance parts (which were apparently dispersed after Bach's death). For new text-critical information, see the appendixes in this book; Marissen, "On Linking Bach's F-Major Sinfonia and His Hunt Cantata," *Bach* (the journal of the Riemenschneider Bach Institute) 23, no. 2 (1992): 31–46; and "Organological Questions and Their Significance in J. S. Bach's Fourth Brandenburg Concerto," *Journal of the American Musical Instrument Society* 17 (1991): 5–52. Another possibility would be that Bach had planned a set from the start and took a very long time in completing it (consider, for example, the *Orgelbüchlein*, which Bach clearly laid out early on in his career but never completed).

[9] For the vast bibliography on this subject, see *Bach-Bibliographie*, ed. Christoph Wolff (Kassel: Merseburger, 1985); and Rosemarie Nestle, "Das Bachschriftum 1981–1985," *Bach-Jahrbuch* 75 (1989): 107–89.

than once played through the entire collection for his student Heinrich Nicolaus Gerber.[10] In part 2 of the *Clavier-Übung*, consisting of *Concerto nach Italiaenischen Gust* (BWV 971, in F major) and *Overture nach Französischer Art* (BWV 831, in B minor), the relationship of systematic oppositions between the two works (Italian vs. French, concerto vs. suite, major vs. minor, flat vs. sharp, and F vs. B in the key pitches) appears to have been at least as important to Bach as the individuality of each of the pieces. Bach presumably went to the inconvenience of transposing the *Overture* down a half-step from an earlier version in C minor in order to emphasize this oppositional relationship between the highly disparate individual works.[11] Christoph Wolff has recently demonstrated that an earlier version of the *Art of Fugue* (Mus. ms. Bach P 200, Staatsbibliothek zu Berlin) was composed near the beginning, not the end, of Bach's late compositional activities.[12] But this discovery that the larger, more familiar version of

---

[10] See *Bach-Dokumente III: Dokumente zum Nachwirken Johann Sebastian Bachs 1750–1800*, ed. Hans-Joachim Schulze (Kassel: Bärenreiter, 1972), p. 476. John Hawkins (1719–89), the English music-historian, mentions Händel's playing in their entirety a set of printed suites by Mattheson right after they appeared (cited in Hans-Joachim Schulze, *Studien zur Bach-Überlieferung im 18. Jahrhundert* [Leipzig: Peters, 1983], p. 52, n. 168). Georg August Griesinger (d. 1828) mentions Haydn's playing through C.P.E. Bach's six Prussian Sonatas when he came upon them (Griesinger, *Biographische Notizen über Joseph Haydn* [Leipzig, 1810], trans. Vernon Gotwals in *Haydn: Two Contemporary Portraits* [Madison: University of Wisconsin Press, 1968], p. 12). It was probably uncommon in the early eighteenth century for ensembles to perform an entire set of concertos, but it was certainly not unheard of. For example, Hawkins also reports that in 1724 at one of the weekly meetings of a gentlemen's academy founded in 1710 "for the encouragement of vocal and instrumental music," there was a concert in which all twelve of Corelli's Op. 6 were played at one sitting (mentioned in Arthur Hutchings, *The Baroque Concerto*, rev. ed. [London: Faber, 1973], pp. 253–54; the report appears in vol. 2 of the Novello edition of Hawkins, *A General History of the Science and Practice of Music: A New Edition, with the Author's Posthumous Notes* [London, 1875], p. 806). Two later examples: C.P.E. Bach's six string symphonies Wq 182/H657–62 were played at one sitting in the home of Johann Georg Büsch (reported in Johann Friedrich Reichardt, "Autobiographie," *Allgemeine musikalische Zeitung* 16 [1814], p. 29); the same went for his symphonies Wq 183/H663–66, according to a letter of 17 August 1776 by Friedrich Gottlieb Klopstock (cited in Hans-Günter Ottenberg, *C.P.E. Bach* [Oxford: Oxford University Press, 1987], p. 172, n. 246). For the purposes of this discussion, it does not matter if complete play-throughs of instrumental collections took place in formal concerts or in more intimate, private (i.e. unofficial) situations.

[11] This C-minor version of BWV 831 is frequently overlooked by students of Bach's music. The 1950 edition of the *Bach-Werke-Verzeichnis* mentioned it but did not provide a special number for it; the 1990 edition has assigned it the number BWV 831a.

[12] See Christoph Wolff, "Zur Chronologie und Kompositionsgeschichte von Bachs Kunst der Fuge," *Beiträge zur Musikwissenschaft* 25 (1983): 130–42 (trans. Alfred Mann

the collection, with its various styles of fugal writing, was composed over an extended period of time (c. 1740–50) has not shaken the view that the last version of the *Art of Fugue* (BWV 1080, printed in 1751 and again in 1752) is a meaningful set. Recent research has also shown that unfamiliar alternate transmissions of early versions to some individual items in the sonatas and partitas for solo violin (BWV 1001–6) and the *Well-Tempered Clavier I* may predate considerably the familiar versions found in Bach's compilations.[13]

The question concerning tonal schemes in Bach's instrumental collections is more complicated and will be explored in some detail farther on. The issue of heterogeneous scoring within an instrumental collection is also not a simple one. For example, discussion of whether or not Bach's *Musical Offering* (BWV 1079), with its varying scorings, is a meaningful set remains controversial.[14] Although I find serious methodological as well as straightforward technical problems in Ursula Kirkendale's much-discussed interpretation favoring the notion of a meaningful set for the *Musical Offering*, I would still argue that the collection is a meaningful set.[15] The necessarily detailed treatment of this problem, however, would bring the present discussion too far afield. I hope, then, that this reading of the diversely scored Brandenburg Concertos will be sufficiently compelling on its own merits.

Some commonly given reasons for interpreting the Brandenburg Concertos as a meaningful set are encountered more often in program notes and other sorts of less formal, unpublished discussions

---

in Wolff, *Bach: Essays on His Life and Music* [Cambridge, Mass.: Harvard University Press, 1991], chap. 20).

[13] See Russell Stinson, "J. P. Kellner's Copy of Bach's Sonatas and Partitas for Violin Solo," *Early Music* 13 (1985): 199–211; Stinson, *The Bach Manuscripts of Johann Peter Kellner and His Circle* (Durham, N.C.: Duke University Press, 1989); and Alfred Dürr, *Zur Frühgeschichte des Wohltemperierten Klaviers I von Johann Sebastian Bach* (Göttingen: Vandenhoeck and Ruprecht, 1984).

[14] The most important treatments of the problem are Christoph Wolff, "New Research on Bach's *Musical Offering*," *Musical Quarterly* 57 (1971): 379–408 (reprinted in Wolff, *Bach: Essays*, chap. 18); and Ursula Kirkendale, "The Source for Bach's *Musical Offering*: The *Institutio oratoria* of Quintilian," *Journal of the American Musicological Society* 33 (1980): 88–141.

[15] Kirkendale, "The Source for Bach's *Musical Offering*"; see Michael Marissen, "The Theological Character of J. S. Bach's *Musical Offering*," *Bach-Studies 2*, ed. Daniel Melamed (Cambridge: Cambridge University Press, forthcoming); and "More Source-Critical Research on J. S. Bach's *Musical Offering*," *Bach* 25, no. 1 (1994): 11–27.

than in academic journal articles and books. The concertos are considered to be linked thematically, since the first movements of all six pieces employ the three notes of the tonic triad in their opening theme. They are also linked stylistically; three of the concertos close with dance movements (the first, third, and sixth), and three close with fugues (the second, fourth, and fifth). And, finally, as Rudolf Eller first pointed out, they are linked tonally by the four keys employed (F major, G major, D major, and B♭ major) to form the two kinds of dominants and double-dominants on either side of C major.[16] These factors all contribute to the unity in diversity said to characterize the collection as a meaningful set.

The usefulness of these kinds of observations is easy to question. Triadic themes are very common in baroque music, many concertos contain dancelike or fugal finales, and there is a great deal of evidence suggesting that Bach often considered the changes of key-signature levels through the circle of fifths per se in modulations to be more significant than the modes to which they correspond. That is, the tonal space between C major and E minor was essentially the same as that between C major and G major, and thus C major was considered to be distantly related to C minor, since the former is sharper by three key-signature levels.[17] Thus, early eighteenth-century German composers probably did not consider it significant that D major and B♭ major are double-dominants of C major, and Bach certainly would not have called them that (Bach was not a follower of Jean-Philippe Rameau's music theories, which, in any case, were not published for the first time until after the Brandenburg Concertos had been compiled[18]).

To come to a richer interpretation of the Brandenburg Concertos as a meaningful set, then, we should not focus so much on unifying factors but, rather, seek a systematic approach in the various elements of contrast within the collection (i.e., with the assumption that coher-

[16] Rudolf Eller, "Einführungen in die Werke des 38. Deutschen Bachfestes: Die Orchester- und Kammermusikwerke," in *38. Deutsches Bachfest der Neuen Bach-Gesellschaft vom 21. bis 26. Juni 1962 in Leipzig: Bach-Fest-Buch* (Leipzig, 1962), pp. 71–96; and "Serie und Zyklus in Bachs Instrumentalsammlungen," in *Bach-Interpretationen: Walter Blankenburg zum 65. Geburtstag*, ed. Martin Geck (Göttingen: Vandenhoeck and Ruprecht, 1969), pp. 126–43, 221–22.

[17] See Eric Chafe, "Key Structure and Tonal Allegory in the Passions of J. S. Bach: An Introduction," *Current Musicology* 31 (1981): 39–54, at p. 39.

[18] Rameau, *Traité de l'Harmonie* (Paris, 1722).

ence and unity are not the same thing). I argue that there are interesting complementary patterns of symmetry and intensification, some that are relatively abstract and others that reinforce these patterns by more overt musical means. Moreover, I argue that in suggesting broader, extramusical issues, these patterns may have more to offer than contrast for its own sake.

A GENERAL aspect that, so far as I am aware, has not been brought up in discussions of the Brandenburg Concertos as a meaningful set is the possible significance of the number of pieces in the collection. The custom of including six pieces in collections of instrumental music in the early eighteenth century is well known, but this practice is almost always taken merely for a convention. The question of why this procedure came so often to be adopted is passed over. The very fact that the word *six* or the numeral 6 appears so conspicuously and so often—typically as the first word—on title pages of these collections suggests that the indication is not merely quantitatively descriptive but somehow more broadly significant.[19]

Already in his *Institutioni harmoniche* of 1558 the theorist Gioseffo Zarlino attached great musical and intellectual significance to the number six. By increasing the number of divisions of the string from the traditional four to six (the *senario*, meaning "six"), Zarlino was able to generate the major third, minor third, and major sixth, which had become considered basic consonances (something not true—not theoretically justified—in earlier theory; in the formal constraints of Zarlino's theory, the minor sixth had to be rationalized as a fourth plus a third). The reason that all this was appealing to Zarlino, not only musically but also intellectually, was that, as had been known for centuries from Pythagorean teaching, six is a "perfect number": it equals the sum of its integer divisions $(1 + 2 + 3 = 6)$.[20]

As Zarlino viewed it, the number six epitomized the formal cause (the "sonorous number") that generated the consonances out of the "sounding body" (e.g., the monochord). The number six was thus also called the "harmonious number." This was not the first time the

[19] This observation provides one point of departure for Klaus-Jürgen Sachs, "Aspekte der numerischen und tonartlichen Disposition instrumentalmusikalischer Zyklen des ausgehenden 17. und beginnenden 18. Jahrhunderts," *Archiv für Musikwissenschaft* 41 (1984): 237–56.
[20] The next three perfect numbers are 28, 496, and 8,128 (see ibid., p. 244).

number six was referred to in this way in music theory. For example, Nicolaus Burtius, in *Musices opusculum* (1487), mentions the perfection of the number six in connection with the six solmization syllables of the hexachord; Johannes Lippius, in *Synopsis musicae novae* (1612), adds a further dimension when he refers to the number six as "primus [numerus] . . . perfectus & mundanus."[21] This worldliness of the number six alludes to God's creating the world in six days. God was believed to have chosen this number to signify the perfection and inner harmony of the creation. That is, in Zarlino's and Lippius's view, the number six does not derive its meaning from the fact that God created the world in six days; rather, God is said to have created the world in six days because this number is inherently significant. Zarlino devotes an entire chapter in his treatise to the importance of the number six in nature and in art and, having accomplished that, outlines the manifestation of the number six in music: there are six "spetie delle Voci" ("Vnisone, Equisone, Consone, Emelle, Dissone & Ecmele"), six "Consonanze" ("Diapason, Diapente, Diatessaron, Ditino, Semiditino, Vnisono"), six "specie di Harmonia" ("Doria, Frigia, Lidia, Mistalidia o Lochrense, Eolia & la Iastia ouero Ionica"), and six "Modi principali detti Autentici, & Sie non principali detti Plagali."[22]

When we consider the long-standing tradition of the significance of the number six with the fact that Johann Gottfried Walther's *Musicalisches Lexicon* (1732) contains an entry for "Numerus perfectus" that cites Lippius's worldliness of the number six indirectly, via Conrad Matthaeis's *Kurtzer, doch ausführlicher Bericht von den Modis Musicus* (1652/1658), we cannot avoid the conclusion that late seventeenth-century and early eighteenth-century composers understood the use of the number six as a *signum perfectionis*.[23] This apparent reference to *perfectio* by the conventional use of the number six in assembling collections of instrumental music contrasts strikingly with the composers' virtually inevitable (i.e., conventional) self-deprecating references within their prefaces to the *imperfectio* of their work.[24] In the preface to his score of the Brandenburg Concertos, Bach falls in line

[21] Ibid.
[22] Ibid., p. 245.
[23] Ibid., p. 246.
[24] Ibid., p. 256.

with the tradition, begging the dedicatee, the margrave of Brandenburg, "most humbly not to judge the imperfection [of his *Six Concerts avec plusieurs Instruments*]" and speaking of "the small talents which heaven has given" him as a composer.[25]

IT WILL APPEAR that both the key structure of the Brandenburg Concertos and their contrasts of ensemble scorings provide patterns of symmetry for the collection. Because this second pattern is much more obviously susceptible to description based on immediate musical experience of the six concertos, however, I will mention it first. The First and Sixth Concertos are ensemble concertos (pieces without consistently detached soloistic subgroups), the Second and Fifth Concertos are concerti grossi (pieces with clearly defined concertino and ripieno groups), and the Third and Fourth Concertos juxtapose the two styles at the center of the collection.[26]

This static pattern of scorings is contradicted, however, with dynamic patterns in varying applications of Vivaldi's fortspinnung-type concerto syntax. Consider first the finales in the ensemble concertos. The dance or dance-derived closing movements to these three concertos successively become more bound to Vivaldian fortspinnung-type syntax.

The contrasts in the last movement of the First Brandenburg Concerto consist primarily of alternations between various small-group

[25] Am.B.78, Staatsbibliothek zu Berlin; facsimile: Peter Wackernagel, ed., *J. S. Bach, Brandenburgische Konzerte: Faksimile nach dem im Besitz der Staatsbibliothek in Berlin befindlichen Autograph* (Leipzig: Peters, 1947).

[26] Bach distinguishes categorically the Second, Fourth, and Fifth Concertos in the manuscript sent to the margrave of Brandenburg by providing them with "in Ripieno" markings for the nonconcertino members, both within the titles and at the headings for the individual lines in the scores. Another minor detail is provided by Ralph Leavis ("J. S. Bach's Violone Parts," *Galpin Society Journal* 30 [1977]: 155–56): in concertos 1, 3, and 6, the violone shares a staff with another instrument, whereas in concertos 2, 4, and 5, the violone has a staff to itself. Bach could, of course, have switched the order of the Third and Fourth Concertos and retained a symmetry in juxtapositions of ensemble concerto to concerto grosso. There is a certain elegance, however, in Bach's assigning the position of "Concerto *3ᵗᵒ*" to the work scored "à *tre* Violini, *tre* Viole, è *tre* Violoncelli, col Baßo per il Cembalo." (On the historical change in reference for the term *concerto grosso* from "large ensemble music" to "concertos with more than one soloist," incidentally, see Erich Reimer, "Concerto/Konzert" (1973) in Hans Heinrich Eggebrecht, ed., *Handwörterbuch der musikalischen Terminologie* [Wiesbaden: F. Steiner, 1972–], p. 11.)

trios and a continually returning large-group minuet. That is, the minuet functions as a sort of tutti "ritornello."

The 12/8 Allegro in the Third Brandenburg Concerto assumes the general character and specific (binary) form of a gigue, but its twelve-measure A section is structured as a vordersatz-fortspinnung moving from G major to D major, followed immediately by a vordersatz-fortspinnung-epilog in D. This large block comes back in its entirety in mm. 17–28 (E minor to B minor) and mm. 37–48 (G major to C major) and thus functions as a sort of "ritornello."

The 12/8 Allegro in the Sixth Brandenburg Concerto assumes the rhythmic character of a gigue, and it opens with a full-fledged ritornello with vordersatz, fortspinnung, and epilog segments. What is presented as a solo theme in mm. 9–12 is, in fact, a rather thinly disguised trio-textured diminution variation on the vordersatz segment of the ritornello (i.e., mm. 9–12 could be superimposed upon mm. 1–4 without any clash). Bach further confounds the conventions of the form in mm. 15–22, an F-major quotation of all eight measures to the ritornello, by juxtaposing trio and full textures not only at the seams of some consecutive ritornello segments but also at internal points of division from other segments. True episodic material (thematically derived, however, from the fortspinnung segment of the ritornello) appears in full-ensemble textures starting in m. 23. Thus with the smaller group's return of the vordersatz segment in m. 32, Bach turns the traditional textural associations of ritornello and episode on their heads. Episodic material that is not at all based on the ritornello appears only in the B section of this da capo movement.

To summarize: as the sizes of Bach's ensembles become progressively smaller in a left-to-right examination of each of the ensemble concertos in the Brandenburg collection, the kinds of textural contrast in the closing movements become more formally sophisticated, and the indebtedness to fortspinnung-type syntax becomes more and more evident.

The three concerto-grosso pieces all close with fugues, each of which becomes successively less bound to fortspinnung-type syntax.

Throughout the Second Brandenburg Concerto, the ripieno section either performs doubling and orchestral basso-continuo functions or it is silent. In the finale, the ripieno hardly ever plays when the fugue subject appears (except at mm. 72 and 119, when the subject is in the bass). Otherwise, the ripieno appears only during the sections of material that Bach structured according to the syntax of fortspinnung and epilog segments (fortspinnung-epilog for mm. 48–57, 97–107, and 126–36; only fortspinnung segment for mm. 79–85). The appearances of the fugue subject at mm. 41, 72, and 119 might even be viewed as "vordersatz" segments preceding the fortspinnung segments of mm. 48, 79, and 126.[27]

The fugue closing the Fourth Brandenburg Concerto shows only slight traces of fortspinnung-type syntax. The one consistent reference to it comes in the vordersatz-fortspinnung organization of the episode quoted at mm. 43, 179, and 193, but the movement still follows a relatively straightforward concerto procedure with marked contrasts of tutti and concertino material.

The giguelike fugue closing the Fifth Brandenburg Concerto shows no obvious traces of fortspinnung-type structure. There are, of course, stretches of sequential and harmonically more static material (as there are in virtually any work from the early eighteenth century), but the organization of the blocks of material is not clearly that of the fortspinnung-type ritornello. In fact, even though there are various markedly set-off sections scored for only the concertino members, the structure of the entire da capo movement does not appear to be organized according to any concerto style involving textural contrast as a formative principle.

Consider, finally, the opening movements of both the ensemble-concerto and concerto-grosso works in the collection.[28] In both types,

---

[27] This is the view of Carl Dahlhaus, "Bachs konzertante Fugen," *Bach-Jahrbuch* 42 (1955): 45–72, at pp. 57–58. Dahlhaus concludes by making the general point that Bach's concerto fugues need not be considered contradictory mixtures of inherently opposed genres (i.e., "strict" fugue and "free" concerto), for the concertante treatment of fugue and the fugal treatment of concerto in Bach's works appears to have transformed both the basic forms in the same way: through modulation for principal thematic material and through thematic development for modulating episodes (p. 65).

[28] Fortspinnung-type syntax plays no role in the slow movements to the ensemble concertos of the collection. There is some use of it, however, in the concerto-grosso works. The Affettuoso of the Fifth Concerto features clear fortspinnung-type organization in its episode of mm. 5–10. Traces of the syntax are found in a continually returning fortspinnung-epilog block in the Andante of the Second Brandenburg Concerto (see mm. 9, 37, and 57), and the Andante of Fourth Concerto has a full-fledged ritornello with vordersatz, fortspinnung, and epilog segments (for a detailed interpretation, see the discussion of this movement in chapter 1).

concerto by concerto, the ritornellos become successively less bound to fortspinnung-type syntax.

In the first ensemble concerto, the First Brandenburg Concerto, the opening ritornello from the first movement outlines a move from F major to C major (mm. 1–6) by means of a very clearly structured vordersatz-fortspinnung-epilog block before closing the ritornello (in m. 13) with further fortspinnung and epilog segments.

The opening ritornello from the first movement of the Third Brandenburg Concerto contains very clearly marked internal divisions, but they cannot be characterized in terms of the vordersatz, fortspinnung, and epilog segmentation of the fortspinnung-type ritornello. Measures 1–3 form a vordersatz segment that divides into two from the middle of m. 2 (the second part of which merely prolongs the dominant), and mm. 4–8 form an epilog that divides into two from the middle of m. 6. In other words, this concerto might be said to employ only the outer segments of the fortspinnung-type ritornello model. (There is no conventional segment of sequential fortspinnung.)

The opening ritornello from the first movement of the Sixth Brandenburg Concerto (mm. 1–17) contains no clearly marked internal divisions with differing thematic characteristics. This ritornello shows no traces whatsoever of sequential fortspinnung-type syntax.[29]

In the first concerto grosso, the Second Brandenburg Concerto, the ritornello from the first movement outlines a very clearly structured vordersatz-fortspinnung-epilog block in three out of four of the ritornello's minor-mode appearances (see mm. 31–39, 75–83, and 94–102 as opposed to mm. 68–72). The opening, major-mode appearance of the ritornello contains only two-part vordersatz and epilog segments. Even though the second half of the vordersatz segment is not designed to be able to lead into the fortspinnung segment (see mm. 68–72), and even though the fortspinnung segment is not designed to work in the major mode (see, for example, m. 33, where the harmony in the second half of the first measure of the fortspinnung segment will not translate grammatically into major),[30] the

[29] In this movement the fortspinnung-type syntax is transferred to a continually returning solo theme (see the detailed discussion of this movement in part 1).

[30] This was pointed out by Laurence Dreyfus, who refers to the set of ritornello segments in the Second Brandenburg Concerto aptly as an "ideal ritornello," so called because the entire set of segments never actually obtains consecutively in the move-

movement may from immediate experience be perceived to have a complete fortspinnung-type ritornello. That is, the ritornello may readily appear to conform to the fortspinnung-type model in spite of the fact that all the segments never show up next to one another in the movement.

In the Fourth Brandenburg Concerto, the opening ritornello from the first movement (mm. 1–83) outlines such an immensely overblown structure that it may not immediately seem to belong to the fortspinnung-type. A tonally closed vordersatz block in G major (mm. 1–13) and an initial fortspinnung (mm. 13–22) lead directly to a literal return of the vordersatz block in D major. An extended passage of three fortspinnung segments (mm. 35–42, 43–47, and 47–56) leads directly to a second literal return of the vordersatz block, now back in the tonic. And, finally, still another fortspinnung (mm. 69–79) joined to a brief epilog (mm. 79–83) closes the ritornello. The only place where there is a fairly clear sense of consecutive vordersatz-fortspinnung-epilog organization within this huge ritornello is in the fourth quarter of its run (mm. 57–83). It is perhaps not surprising, then, that this apparently stylistically complete section from within the ritornello comes back in this specific layout three times outside of the opening and closing ritornellos (see mm. 137–57, 209–35, and 323–44), whereas the extended sequential passage of fortspinnung segments comes back in only one internal ritornello (see mm. 263–85). But because the fortspinnung segment that consistently precedes the epilog is so strongly subdominant-oriented (as opposed to conventional fortspinnung segments, which are tonic- or dominant-oriented), each quotation of the vordersatz-fortspinnung-epilog section from within the extended ritornello may be experienced as musically incomplete, in spite of the presence of all three categories of fortspinnung-type ritornello division. The ritornello would not work if the piece were set up to start in m. 57 and close with mm. 345–400 having been removed from the da capo. As a result, the sense of the fortspinnung-type model prevails somewhat less forcefully in the Fourth Brandenburg Concerto than in the Second.

In the Fifth Brandenburg Concerto, the ritornello from the first movement (mm. 1–9) has clearly marked internal divisions, but they

ment. See Dreyfus, "J. S. Bach's Concerto Ritornellos and the Question of Invention," *Musical Quarterly* 71 (1985): 327–58, at pp. 346–51.

cannot be characterized precisely according to the terms of fortspin-nung-type syntax.[31] The ritornello has what might be labeled vorder-satz (mm. 1–2) and epilog segments (in mm. 3–7 and 7–9), but there is no conventional segment of sequential fortspinnung.

THE SYMMETRICAL organization of the Brandenburg Concertos by means of two formal categories (ensemble works without a segregated ripieno and concerto-grosso works) may seem striking and unusual. Alternating two types of scoring throughout a collection of concertos was not, however, a new idea with Bach. For example, the Op. 2 *Sinfonie e Concerti a cinque* of Tomaso Albinoni—a collection that Bach probably knew—contains, despite the general title, separate works called "Sonata I," "Concerto I," "Sonata II," "Concerto II," and so forth, up to "Concerto VI."[32] And the Op. 8 *Concerti grossi* of Giuseppe Torelli, a collection Bach may have known, also juxtaposes old and new styles.[33] The first six pieces are largely string-ensemble works, and last six are what came to be known as violin concertos.[34]

When these collections were assembled, the word *concerto* still had two rather different meanings. Ensemble works would have been thought more likely to manifest the one notion of concerto, and concerto-grosso works the other. But in order to approach properly the details of this issue and their significance for the Brandenburg Concertos, we need first to focus at some length on the tonal scheme of Bach's collection.

[31] Fortspinnung-type syntax appears, rather, in the solo theme of mm. 9–19 (vorder-satz segment in mm. 9–11 and 11–13, fortspinnung in 13–16, and epilog in 16–19), which reappears in mm. 110–21.

[32] The isolated continuo part cataloged in the first edition of the *Bach-Werke-Verzeichnis* as BWV Anh. 23 had been believed to belong to a lost Bach concerto in E minor, but it was recently discovered that the part is merely Bach's copy, perhaps prepared during his tenure in Weimar, of Albinoni's Op. 2, no. 2 (see Schulze, *Studien zur Bach-Überlieferung*, p. 28). Also, Johann Gottfried Walther, who along with Bach appears to have been commissioned to prepare arrangements of string concertos for Prince Johann Ernst of Weimar, made keyboard arrangements of the fourth and fifth concertos from Albinoni's Op. 2.

[33] Reinhard Goebel, "J. S. Bach: Die Brandenburgischen Konzerte," *Concerto*, no. 8 (1987): 16–18, suggests that it is not coincidental that the head motive of the opening movement of the First Brandenburg Concerto quotes Torelli's Op. 8, no. 2 (except that there is a mode switch from minor to major). Walther also made keyboard arrangements of pieces from this collection.

[34] Hutchings, *The Baroque Concerto*, p. 96. Torelli's Op. 5 collection also places two styles in juxtaposition.

Although by present-day standards we do not have any obvious evidence of a dispositional scheme in the tonal layout of the six Brandenburg Concertos, we may come closer to a rationalization of Bach's tonal structure by refining Eller's observation on Bach's use of both kinds of dominants and double-dominants around C major,[35] reformulating the idea in terms of some branches of contemporary German music theory. Bach may not have thought the First Brandenburg Concerto was related to the Sixth because the central triad in the former's key (F major) could function as a dominant chord to the latter's (B♭ major), but he would have considered the two keys to be quite closely related, for he appears to have considered that key-signature levels (how many sharps or flats a signature contained) indicate distance from a central area without any accidentals in its key signature.

An outline of this kind of tonal thinking can be found in Johann David Heinichen's *Neu erfundene und gründliche Anweisung* (Hamburg, 1711).[36] While Heinichen shows a very modern outlook, being the first to formulate a musical circle with all twenty-four possible major and minor keys,[37] he also harks back to older, hexachord-related theory, in which the *cantus durus* and *mollis* were frequently referred to as *genera*, when he describes the sharp keys of his circle as *Genus Chromaticum* and the flat keys as *Genus Enharmonicum*. Heinichen measures keys according to their distance from the extremes (*Extrema*) of his circle. Thus C minor is by nature more enharmonic than G minor because it is closer to the *Extremo Enharmonico*, B♭ minor, a key that he says is "hardly usable." According to Heinichen, the farther one moves through the key-signature levels in the musical circle away from C major, "the easiest key in music," the more "difficult" the key.[38]

[35] See n. 16.

[36] Regarding Bach's and Prince Leopold's personal connections with Heinichen, see Marissen, "J. S. Bach's Brandenburg Concertos as a Meaningful Set," p. 225, n. 37.

[37] See Chafe, "J. S. Bach's *St. Matthew Passion*: Aspects of Planning, Structure, and Chronology," *Journal of the American Musicological Society* 35 (1982): 49–114, at p. 58, n. 16.

[38] The summary of this aspect of Heinichen's theory is taken from ibid., pp. 59–60. Chafe also points out that Andreas Werckmeister describes the nonharmonic relation as a place where "one in a flash falls from one *Genus* into the other" (*Harmonologica musica* [Frankfurt, 1702], par. 67). See also the discussion of Heinichen's 1711 treatise in Joel Lester, "The Recognition of Major and Minor Keys in German Theory: 1680–1730," *Journal of Music Theory* 22 (1978): 65–103, at pp. 78–82; and Lester, *Between Modes and Keys: German Theory, 1592–1802* (Stuyvesant, N.Y.: Pendragon Press, 1989).

The four keys traversed in the Brandenburg Concertos, all major-mode (F–G–D–Bb), are symmetrically related to each other as a set; they extend in both directions through the musical circle from an ideal (i.e., nonobtaining) tonal center of C major to key-signature levels with two accidentals. To employ the terms of the *Genera*, the one extreme key in Bach's collection is as chromatic as the other extreme key is enharmonic. We will pursue the potential interpretive significance of this idea later on in this discussion.

Bach's ordering of these four key pitches can be rationalized in the Brandenburg Concertos by reference to the hexachords of solmization. Solmization helped musicians to sing correct intervals by marking semitones with the *mi/fa* of the hexachords. Behind the *mi/fa* lies the idea that scales generated from successive perfect fifths never close into perfect circles. That is, the term *ambitus* (literally, "circle") referred to the range and pitch set of a mode, and a *mi* and a *fa* constitute the extremes that meet at the points of (imperfect) closure to the circles. For example, in a natural-hexachord circle (F–C–G–D–A–E) the extremes are E/F. In a diatonic-octave (two-hexachord) circle (F–C–G–D–A–E–B or Bb–F–C–G–D–A–E) the extremes are F/B or Bb/E, and in the gamut (three-hexachord) circle Bb–F–C–G–D–A–E–B the extremes are Bb/B.[39]

Before exploring their role in the key scheme of the Brandenburg Concertos, we ought perhaps to point out briefly that the hexachords are known to have played a significant role in Bach's musical thinking as both a child and an adult. A great number of music handbooks containing elements of notation, solmization, some rudimentary theory, and singing exercises were written for use in the *Lateinschule* and *Lyceum*,[40] educational institutions that Bach attended in Eisenach and Ohrdruf. When the mature Bach compiled his own rules of thoroughbass for use by his students, he quoted extensively from Friederich Erhardt Niedt's *Musicalische Handleitung* (Hamburg,

---

[39] See Chafe, "Allegorical Music: The 'Symbolism' of Tonal Language in the Bach Canons," *Journal of Musicology* 3 (1984): 340–62, at p. 359.

[40] See Lester, "Major-Minor Concepts and Modal Theory in Germany, 1592–1680," *Journal of the American Musicological Society* 30 (1977): 208–53, at pp. 235–43. On the other hand, there are some instruction books from the 1690s that strongly recommend the use in singing exercises only of letter names (e.g., Johann Georg Ahle, *Kurze doch deutliche Anleitung zu der lieblich- und löblichen Singekunst* [Mühlhausen, 1690]; my thanks to John Butt, University of California, Berkeley, for pointing this out to me).

1710), vol. 1.[41] Niedt's presentation of key signatures follows the pitches of the three hexachords in the gamut, with both a major and a minor key for each keynote (C, c, D, d, E, e, F, f, G, g, A, a, B♭, b♭, B, b). Niedt's scheme, strikingly (from a modern perspective), avoids a frequently used key like E♭ major but does present difficult keys like B♭ minor and B major.

Several of Bach's works from around the time the Brandenburg Concertos were assembled use keynotes from the hexachords in forming their tonal schemes. The solo violin sonatas and partitas (BWV 1001–6) employ the six pitches of the hard hexachord (G, A, B, C, D, and E). The keys of Bach's scheme here are not intrinsically (i.e., functionally) related to each other; that is, Bach does not present tonic, dominant, and subdominant keys and their relatives, as for example in the arrangement a–C–e–G–b–D. Rather, Bach's keys are related by imposition from without in the intervallically symmetrical scheme g–b–a–d–C–E (i.e., the intervals between successive key pitches are major third, minor seventh, perfect fourth, minor seventh, and major third). The key notes of the first version of the six sonatas for violin and obbligato harpsichord (BWV 1014–19a) offer broader and more complex relationships, also imposed from without, by means of the symmetrical and gamut-based scheme b–A–E–c–f–G. The keynotes of the sixth and first sonatas correspond to the *ut* and *mi* of the hard hexachord, the keynotes of the fifth and second sonatas correspond to the *ut* and *mi* of the soft hexachord, and the keynotes of the fourth and third sonatas correspond to the *ut* and *mi* of the natural hexachord. Furthermore, if the *ut* is major, the *mi* is minor (and vice versa). Even in the *Well-Tempered Clavier I*, whose tonal scheme is neither functionally based nor remotely hexachord-based, the language of solmization is featured conspicuously on Bach's title page.[42] There, he refers to moving through all twenty-four keys "both as regards the *tertia major* or *Ut Re Mi* and as concerns the *tertia minor* or *Re Mi Fa*."[43]

[41] Bach's *Vorschriften und Grundsätze zum vierstimmigen Spielen des General-Bass* have been printed in Philipp Spitta, *Johann Sebastian Bach* (Leipzig, 1880), vol. 2, pp. 913–50.

[42] Mus. ms. Bach P 415, Staatsbibliothek zu Berlin.

[43] Hans T. David and Arthur Mendel, eds., *The Bach Reader: A Life of Johann Sebastian Bach in Letters and Documents*, rev. ed. (New York: Norton, 1966), p. 85, suggest that Bach's somewhat complicated description of what we today know simply as major and minor was necessitated by the fact that these terms (in German, *Dur* and *Moll*) had not

The key scheme of the Brandenburg Concertos, F–F–G–G–D–B♭, presents four out of the six pitches in the hexachord F–G–A–B♭–C–D, that is, the soft hexachord. An ordering principle may emerge by reference to the model provided by the circle of successive fifths (B♭–F–C–G–D–A). Bach commences on F and moves clockwise through the circle by skipping over C, providing G and D, skipping over A, and closing the circle with B♭.

Several questions arise when we look at Bach's key scheme in this way. If the key scheme is based on the pitches of the soft hexachord, it is not readily apparent why Bach would skip over two key notes and present two others twice, or why the scheme would involve only the major mode. Bach's procedure can be read interestingly in light of the keys employed in the best known and most admired collection of concertos in early eighteenth-century Germany, Antonio Vivaldi's *L'Estro Armonico* (Op. 3). As has been mentioned several times, Vivaldi's Op. 3 concertos provided the most dramatic impulse for the change around 1713 in the surface characteristics of Bach's musical style in all genres; and the influence on the Brandenburg Concertos specifically of the fortspinnung-type concerto model that Bach encountered in the *L'Estro Armonico* collection has already been discussed at some length. The same sorts of observations that were made about the relationships between Vivaldi's relatively impulsive and Bach's more systematic approach to concerto procedure can be broadened here to include also the tonal orderings in their collections.

The concertos in Vivaldi's *L'Estro Armonico* employ the keys D (twice), d, E, e, F, G, g, A, a (twice), and b. In other words, Vivaldi uses five out of the six key notes in the hard and natural hexachords, the former being restricted to representation in the minor mode (g, a, b, d, e) and the latter to the major mode (D, E, F, G, A). Looking at the key pitches in this way neatly accounts for the absence in Vivaldi's collection of the common key of B♭ major and for the presence of the then relatively extreme key of E major. It also accounts for the absence of F minor. In both hexachords, Vivaldi skips over the pitch C while providing the second pitch of the respective hexachords twice

<hr>

yet come into general use. Lester, "The Recognition of Major and Minor Keys," p. 96, n. 9, has shown this observation to be incorrect; decades earlier, Werckmeister had complained that *Dur* and *Moll* were in such common use that he would accept them even though he did not approve of them.

(D major and A minor each occur twice). Charting Vivaldi's keys from left to right through the collection, one finds only a tidy appearance involving the continuous juxtaposition of major and minor before a switch at the end to close the collection in major (D–g–G–e–A–a–F–a–D–b–d–E), an order that by no means reflects highly rationalized planning.[44]

Bach's Brandenburg Concertos may be seen at the level of tonal scheme to form a significant relationship to their Vivaldian precursors. Whereas the key pitches of Vivaldi's collection can be associated with the hard and natural hexachords, the key pitches of Bach's collection can be associated with the soft hexachord. Thus, the key notes of the two collections together form the three hexachords comprising the gamut, the ancient musical symbol of totality. I am suggesting, in other words, that in some broad sense Bach's Brandenburg Concertos appear to complete Vivaldi's *L'Estro Armonico*.

Although the word *gamut* did not retain its meaning of totality or full range in the German language (as it did in English), there is among the individually transmitted Bach canons one piece with an inscription that indicates Bach still thought of the musical gamut as a symbol of completion. His title *Fa Mi et Mi Fa est tota Musica* for the canon BWV 1078 ("Leipzig, 1 March 1749") expresses essentially the same idea.[45]

There is, incidentally, no reason for doubting that Bach was familiar with Vivaldi's collection in its entirety. Like so many other musicians and patrons throughout Europe, Prince Johann Ernst of Weimar got fully caught up in the "Vivaldi fever" of Op. 3: around 1713 he forwarded to the Weimar court, where Bach was then employed, a large quantity of music purchased during his travels in the Netherlands, where *L'Estro Armonico* had recently been published; he soon took up composition lessons in this new concerto style from Johann Gottfried Walther, Bach's Weimar relative; and, at the same time, he apparently commissioned Walther and Bach to arrange solo keyboard versions of Vivaldi's and others' concertos.[46] It may well be

[44] This is based on the first edition (the one Bach would have known), which Vivaldi published around 1711 with Roger in Amsterdam. A later edition by Walsh in London changes the order of the concertos (see Peter Ryom, *Répertoire des Oeuvres d'Antonio Vivaldi: Les compositions instrumentales* [Copenhagen: Engstrøm & Sødring, 1986], pp. 16–19).

[45] See Chafe, "Allegorical Music," pp. 358–60.

[46] See the studies by Schulze cited here on p. 11, n. 1.

that the burden of proof lies with scholars who believe that Bach was familiar with only part of Vivaldi's collection. Intriguingly, the (in some respects unreliable) report of Johann Nikolaus Forkel on Bach's reception of the Op. 3 refers to Bach's knowledge of Vivaldi's entire set: "[Bach] so often heard [the Op. 3 concertos] praised as admirable compositions that he conceived the happy idea of arranging them all for his clavier [sie sämmtlich für sein Clavier einzurichten]."[47] Most of Bach's keyboard transcriptions of concertos survive in a small number of later, secondary manuscripts that do not appear to be based on early sources. The one surviving autograph, the Concerto in D minor, BWV 596 (based on Vivaldi's Op. 3, no. 11), is by far the oldest extant concerto copy, which in itself might suggest that there were more arrangements by Bach than we know about.[48] According to the current state of research on the possible exemplars to Bach's surviving solo-keyboard arrangements of five *L'Estro Armonico* concertos, there is nothing to indicate that his exemplars were derived from somewhere other than Vivaldi's 1711 printed versions of the concertos.[49] (The manuscript scores used by Bach to make his keyboard arrangements would have been prepared from Vivaldi's printed parts.) Russell Stinson has shown that Bach's students continued to make arrangements from Vivaldi's Op. 3 under their teacher's supervision in Leipzig (including ones for which no corresponding Bach arrangements survive).[50] Kirsten Beißwenger goes on from this and from the fact that Bach arranged in Leipzig the B-minor concerto, Op. 3, no. 10, to suggest that Bach himself therefore probably owned a print of Op. 3 (an alternative, perhaps more likely, suggestion would be that Bach owned a set of scores prepared from the Weimar court's printed orchestral parts).[51]

---

[47] See Forkel, *Ueber Johann Sebastian Bachs Leben, Kunst und Kunstwerke* (Leipzig, 1802), ed. Walther Vetter (Berlin: Henschel, 1966), p. 50; *The Bach Reader*, p. 317.

[48] See Peter Williams, *The Organ Music of J. S. Bach* (Cambridge: Cambridge University Press, 1980), vol. 1, p. 283.

[49] See Karl Heller, ed., *NBA* 4.8: *Bearbeitungen fremder Werke*, Kritischer Bericht (Kassel: Bärenreiter, 1980), p. 14; and Schulze, *Studien zur Bach-Überlieferung*, pp. 159 and 164.

[50] Stinson, "The 'Critischer Musicus' as Keyboard Transcriber? Scheibe, Bach, and Vivaldi," *Journal of Musicological Research* 9 (1990): 255–71.

[51] Beißwenger, *Johann Sebastian Bachs Notenbibliothek* (Kassel: Bärenreiter, 1992), p. 42. It is also well worth mentioning that there is evidence suggesting Bach was interested in owning complete sets of published music per se. For example, after having copied some individual items in Charles François Dieupart's *Six Suittes de clavessin*

For other examples of gamut-based relationships between two collections of instrumental music, this time both by the same composer, consider Bach's employment of specifically the eight key pitches from the three hexachords in the gamut for the tonal scheme of his *Clavier-Übung*, parts 1 and 2.[52] Bach was probably following his Leipzig predecessor Johann Kuhnau, whose two-part *Clavier-Übung* (Leipzig, 1689 and 1692) presents fourteen *Partien* in the tonal layout C–D–E–F–G–A–B♭/c–d–e–f–g–a–b, to which is appended (*"benebenst . . . auffgesetzet"*) an ensemble-style sonata in B♭ scored for solo harpsichord. The six partitas in Bach's *Clavier-Übung* (Leipzig, 1731), with the series B♭–c–a–D–G–e (related intervallically by rising second, falling third, rising fourth, falling fifth, rising sixth), do not as yet spell out a single hexachord. Bach apparently considered this collection of partitas to be self-contained, for there are six pieces (suggesting the earlier-mentioned notion of *signum perfectionis*) that are designated "OPUS 1" (the only use of uppercase letters on Bach's title page). Bach presumably intended to place the collection into a significant relationship with a subsequent compilation, his *Zweyter Theil der Clavier-Übung* (Leipzig, 1735). The F major of the Italian Concerto that opens this collection (related intervallically by falling seventh to the E minor of the sixth Partita) completes the smaller, diatonic-octave circle of the soft and natural hexachords (i.e., the circle of key pitches B♭–F–C–G–D–A–E).[53] The B minor (related intervallically by tritone to the Italian Concerto) of the French Overture provides the one

---

(Amsterdam, n.d.) from manuscript copies, Bach evidently went to great lengths to acquire each of the remaining pieces. He copied them several years later from a newly obtained exemplar of the printed set of six suites. My thanks to Kirsten Beißwenger (Bach-Institut, Göttingen) for pointing this out to me; see also *Johann Sebastian Bachs Notenbibliothek*, p. 202.

[52] My thanks to Eric Chafe, Brandeis University, for pointing out to me his rationalization of the tonal scheme to Bach's *Clavier-Übung*, parts 1 and 2. Chafe's interpretation takes into consideration the significance of many factors besides the tonal scheme. For the purposes of this discussion, I am mentioning only the aspect of his interpretation that has to do with key-pitches.

[53] Bach's earlier plan evidently was to include in the collection of partitas a seventh work (which logically would have been in F major). Starting in 1726, Bach published the partitas singly in sequence before issuing the edition containing the six partitas in 1731. From an advertisement accompanying the appearance of the fifth partita, we learn that *two* more partitas were planned for publication (see *Bach-Dokumente II: Fremdschriftliche und gedruckte Dokumente zum Lebensgeschichte Johann Sebastian Bachs 1685–1750*, ed. Werner Neumann and Hans-Joachim Schulze [Kassel: Bärenreiter, 1969], p. 202).

pitch missing from the hard hexachord and thereby completes the circle of the gamut (B♭–F–C–G–D–A–E–B). That is, in this sense the *Clavier-Übung*, part 2, "completes" the *Clavier-Übung*, part 1.

As for the key scheme in the Brandenburg Concertos, the reason, in this interpretation, for Bach's traversing only the major mode and for skipping over two key notes of the soft hexachord while presenting two others twice may also be provided in the posited relationship between Bach's collection and Vivaldi's Op. 3. If Vivaldi uses only the minor mode for keys based on the hard hexachord and only the major mode for keys based on the natural hexachord, Bach might, wishing to relate his six concertos to Vivaldi's in a significant way, choose a single mode for key pitches to outline the soft hexachord. The minor mode would not do, for the key of B♭ minor was too impractical for ensemble music (there are no known eighteenth-century concertos in B♭ minor). Upon choosing the major mode, Bach may have skipped over A major, not to avoid any practical difficulty with the key (there is a considerable number of eighteenth-century concertos in A major) but to allow for a symmetrical relationship within the six concertos of enharmonicism to chromaticism in the sense of the *Genera*. That is, without the A, the major-mode keys on the pitches of the soft hexachord will extend to signatures of two flats and two sharps; and just as both Vivaldi's hexachords lacked the C, Bach's scheme skips over C. But whereas in Vivaldi the absence appears arbitrary (unsystematic), in Bach the absence of C allows it to act as the ideal (nonobtaining) center in a symmetrical (systematic) relationship of sharps and flats in the key signatures. In spite of the absence of two key pitches in Bach's outlining of the hexachord, an ordering pattern (a systematic approach), starting on F, is recognizable from a clockwise procession through the carefully selected members of the circle of successive fifths B♭–F–[C]–G–D–[A]. Vivaldi's ordering of the key notes in his Op. 3, however, shows no recognizable pattern. In comparison to Bach's, Vivaldi's approach throughout is unsystematic.

With the absence of C major in the Brandenburg Concertos, Bach does not allow for a crossover from sharps to flats via a neutral key containing no accidentals in its key signature. In other words, the collection may be viewed to place concertos in flats against concertos in sharps. In recent studies of tonality and meaning in Bach's vocal works, scholars have shown, for example, that the juxtaposition of sharp and flat keys unites musico-allegorical considerations with theology in Bach's passion settings.[54] It is possible, in fact, to chart associations and progressions within the series of six Brandenburg Concertos by relating contrasts between the pieces in sharps and flats in terms of alternate meanings of the word *concerto.*

Writers on music do not agree on the etymology of the word *concerto.* Some suggest that it comes from *conserere,* "to consort," and others (citing particularly the third part of Michael Praetorius, *Syntagma Musicum* [Wolfenbüttel, 1619]) from *concertare,* "to compete." Still others point out that in classical and medieval usage *concertare* has a second meaning, "to act together" or "to work hard with a common purpose."[55] The notions of concerto as both consorting and competing are featured in the description of concerto by Bach's contemporary Johann Mattheson, whose definition is later quoted in Walther's *Lexicon:*[56]

Concertos, broadly speaking, are [musical] gatherings and *collegia musica* [i.e., what we today call "concerts"], but in a strict manner of speaking, this word is often taken to mean chamber music for both voices and instruments (i.e., a piece actually so named [Mattheson's term *Cammer-Musik* would include music for private devotions]), and, more strictly still, pieces for strings [*Violin*

---

[54] See Chafe, "Key Structure and Tonal Allegory," and Chafe, *Tonal Allegory in the Vocal Music of J. S. Bach* (Berkeley and Los Angeles: University of California Press, 1991).

[55] See the summary in Hutchings, *The Baroque Concerto,* pp. 26–27; see also David Boyden, "When Is a Concerto Not a Concerto?" *Musical Quarterly* 43 (1957): 220–32.

[56] See Mattheson, *Das Neu-eröffnete Orchestre* (Hamburg, 1713), pp. 173–74; translated in Michael Talbot, *Vivaldi,* rev. ed. (New York: Schirmer, 1993), p. 107. Hutching's assertion that no "eighteenth-century writer . . . speaks of strife or competition among the participants" is therefore incorrect (*The Baroque Concerto,* p. 26). Further examples of Mattheson's understanding of *concerto* from German writers in the first half of the eighteenth century, including Bach's student, Johann Adolph Scheibe, are provided by Reimer, "Concerto/Konzert," pp. 9–11. I should point out that for the purposes of the present interpretation, we are concerned with German-baroque composers' understanding of the term, not so much with whether their usage was etymologically correct. For a detailed study of what may have been the actual etymology of "concerto," see Siegfried Kross, "Concerto—Concertare und Conserere," in Carl Dahlhaus, ed., *Bericht über den internationalen musikwissenschaftlichen Kongreß Leipzig 1966* (Kassel: Bärenreiter, 1970), pp. 216–20. We know, incidentally, that Walther had begun work on his *Lexicon* already while both he and Bach, a relative, were living in Weimar (see Eggebrecht, "Walthers Musikalisches Lexicon in seiner terminologischen Partien," *Acta Musicologica* 29 [1957]: 10–27). We also know that Bach acted as Walther's Leipzig agent for the sale of the *Lexicon* (see *Bach-Dokumente II,* p. 191).

Sachen] composed in such a way that each part in turn comes into prominence and *vies, as it were*, with the other parts [mit den andern Stimmen *gleichsam um die Wette* spielet—emphasis mine]; hence also in such pieces and others where only the uppermost part is dominant, and where among several violins one, called *Violino concertino*, stands out on account of its especially rapid playing.

It may appear from this quotation in isolation that Mattheson was not aware of contradictory definitions of the same genre but was really talking about different categories commonly called concerto, the one involving "sounding together," namely church music for voices and instruments, and the other involving "competition," namely instrumental music for soloists versus ensemble. Both understandings of concerto, however, were applied during Bach's lifetime to vocal and instrumental music.[57] In a subsequent discussion of vocal concerto, Mattheson refers clearly to the notion of competing;[58] and in Tomaso Albinoni's *Sinfonie e Concerti a cinque*, Op. 2, an instrumental collection that Bach probably knew,[59] there is a reference to concerto as "sounding together": Albinoni applies the designation not to the solo violin part—here called simply *violino primo*, where we might expect *violino concertato* ("the competing violin")—but to the ensemble violin, here called the *violino de concerto* ("the violin of the consort").[60]

Just as earlier we found intensification patterns in varying applications of Vivaldi's fortspinnung-type concerto syntax coordinated with Bach's symmetrical juxtaposition of types of scoring, we may also find intensification patterns of varying "concerto" treatments coordinated into Bach's symmetrical key structure. On the one hand, the three Brandenburg concertos with flats in their key signatures, if read from left to right through the collection, appear concerto by concerto, as they achieve greater enharmonicism in the sense of the *Genera* (i.e., move from one flat to two flats), to become somewhat more concertolike in the sense of the definition "to consort." It is really a matter of what was most strongly emphasized within the music, however, since all six concertos, to varying degrees, can of course be characterized in terms of both definitions of concerto. On the other hand, the three

---

[57] See Reimer, "Concerto/Konzert."

[58] Mattheson, *Der Vollkommene Capellmeister* (Hamburg, 1739), pp. 221–22, quoted in Reimer, "Concerto/Konzert," p. 8.

[59] See n. 32.

[60] See Reimer, "Concerto/Konzert," p. 2.

concertos with sharps in their key signatures, if read from left to right through the collection, appear concerto by concerto, as they achieve greater chromaticism in the sense of the *Genera* (i.e., move from one sharp to two sharps), to become somewhat more concertolike in the sense of the definition "to compete."

Consider first the enharmonic (flats) concertos. The First Brandenburg Concerto shows signs of overt struggle for certain instruments to reach or to be brought away from the center of attention, specifically by the seigneurial horns, instruments that in the first movement are gradually brought down from their outdoor associations of the aristocratic hunt to become equal to the other instruments, all adopting nonidiomatic counterpoint. This sense of struggle holds especially true for the inglorious *violino piccolo concertato*, which in the third movement is never allowed, despite continual striving, to become convincingly the central soloist promised by its title.[61]

An early version of the First Brandenburg Concerto survives as the Sinfonia in F major, BWV 1046a (formerly BWV 1071). This version lacks the third movement and the polonaise of the Brandenburg Concerto, lacks a part for violino piccolo (i.e., one that either doubles or takes the place of the first violin in the corresponding movements of the Brandenburg Concerto), and assigns the oboe line of the final trio to the violins. The revisions in scoring and overall form may be seen to strengthen within the series of Brandenburg Concertos the earlier-mentioned pattern coordinating greater enharmonicism with an increased *conserere* ("to consort") sense of concerto. In particular, the addition of the third movement, with its obbligato part for violino piccolo, gives the First Brandenburg Concerto the least consortlike character of the enharmonic concertos in Bach's collection. For the purposes of this interpretation, then, the question of whether the First Brandenburg Concerto as an isolated work ought to be considered a compositional improvement over the F-major Sinfonia is moot.[62]

The Second Brandenburg Concerto shows fewer signs of struggle

[61] See the detailed discussion of this concerto in part 1.

[62] In fact, the possibility that Bach continued to perform the Sinfonia version of the concerto in Leipzig cannot be excluded. The earliest surviving manuscript, a score copied by Christian Friedrich Penzel (Mus. ms. Bach P 1061, Staatsbibliothek zu Berlin), stems from a set of orchestral parts, apparently of Leipzig origin (see Schulze, "Johann Sebastian Bachs Konzerte—Fragen der Überlieferung und Chronologie," in Bach-Studien 6, *Beiträge zum Konzertschaffen Johann Sebastian Bachs,* ed. Peter Ansehl [Leipzig: VEB Breitkopf and Härtel, 1981], pp. 9–26, at p. 17).

and competition. The soloists are treated so equally that, unusually for Bach, there is no essential differentiation in the style of writing for the four treble instruments, despite the fact that they represent a wide repertory of different ways of producing sound in the early eighteenth century (brass-woodwind-reed-string: trumpet-recorder-oboe-violin). The ripieno section of the ensemble performs only a doubling or an orchestral basso-continuo function whenever it appears; nothing contrapuntally or harmonically essential would be lost if the ripieno string parts were removed and the piece were performed with only the four soloists accompanied by Bach's *Violoncello e Cembalo al unisono* line.[63] The relatively uncharged relationship between the (equal) soloists and the (dispensable) ripieno is all the more remarkable when we consider that the four soloists might, at the time the Brandenburg Concertos were compiled, readily have been associated with the *Stadtpfeifer*, the municipal musician's organization that was constantly envious of courtly musical establishments, a group that required apprentices to pass an examination in brass, woodwind, reed, string playing.[64] The concerto appears upon close historical consideration to be rather uncourtly in some respects.

[63] This is not to say, however, that there must have been an earlier version without the ripieno strings. Unlike in the well-known case of the Concerto in C major for two harpsichords with strings (BWV 1061) or without strings (BWV 1061a), there is no manuscript evidence for an earlier scoring without the ripieno in the Second Brandenburg Concerto. Laurence Dreyfus has reported that the continuo section of the Second Brandenburg Concerto had earlier required a violone (in the 8' register) as the sole string instrument with readings undifferentiated from the harpsichord continuo part, and that Bach designed for the margrave of Brandenburg a new version of the piece with differentiated bass parts in which the cello takes over the readings of the previous violone part (see *Bach's Continuo Group: Players and Practices in His Vocal Works* [Cambridge, Mass.: Harvard University Press, 1987], p. 149). Neither of these observations is supported, however, by the early manuscripts. The set of orchestral parts in question, copied by C. F. Penzel in the 1750s (Mus. ms. Bach St 637, Staatsbibliothek zu Berlin), does in fact differentiate the bass parts, in the same way that Bach does in his score for the margrave of Brandenburg. Since the score in question, also in Penzel's handwriting (Mus. ms. Bach P 1062, likewise Berlin), was copied from St 637—not, as might be expected, the other way around—it has very limited text-critical value. That is, P 1062 reproduces idiosyncratic errors of St 637 and transmits others not found in St 637; also, Penzel amalgamated the bass parts of St 637 onto one line in P 1062, where they are differentiated in only some cases, mostly within the Allegro assai.

[64] Consider in this regard Bach's letter of 24 July 1745 recommending that Carl Friedrich Pfaffe be promoted from apprentice to assistant among the Leipzig *Stadtpfeifer*. Bach states that at the trial examination "[Pfaffe] performed quite well and to the applause of all those present on all the instruments that are customarily em-

If the Second Brandenburg Concerto is somewhat more consort-like than the First, the Sixth may be seen to continue this pattern by coordinating its greater enharmonicism in the sense of the *Genera* (i.e., move to two flats) with a reduction in scoring. Here, the ensemble consists of a handful of low stringed instruments with continuo harpsichord. In other words, the piece is set quite literally for a small "consort." The prestigious, traditionally nonorchestral, soloistic violas da gamba here serve either a ripieno function or a clearly secondary solo function, while the humble, traditionally orchestral violas assume the function of principal soloists.[65] Thus, perhaps somewhat surprisingly (given the extreme contrast with switched roles for the instruments), there are no signs of struggle for the center of attention.

Consider next the three Brandenburg concertos with sharps in their key signatures, which, as mentioned earlier, if read from left to right through the collection, appear concerto by concerto, as they achieve greater chromaticism in the sense of the *Genera* (i.e., move from one sharp to two sharps), to become somewhat more concer-tolike in the sense of the definition "to compete." As in the discussion of concertos with flats in their key signatures, it is really a matter of what was emphasized within the music, however, because all six of the concertos, to varying degrees, can be characterized in terms of both definitions of concerto.

The Third Brandenburg Concerto is scored for an ensemble of strings: three violins, three violas, three cellos, and continuo (harpsichord and violone). There is a great deal of textural contrasting between various subgroups and the entire ensemble (e.g., by the three violins, the three violas, or the three cellos and also by single members), but there is no real sense of struggle associated with any single part of the ensemble's attempting to take the center of attention. Bach appears here to have leveled the conventional stratification of the eighteenth-century string ensemble. Rather than feature active violin lines, relatively active bass lines, and much less active

---

ployed by the Town Pipers, namely: violin, oboe, transverse flute, horn, and the remaining bass instruments." See *Bach-Dokumente I: Schriftstücke von der Hand Johann Sebastian Bachs*, ed. Werner Neumann and Hans-Joachim Schulze (Kassel: Bärenreiter, 1963), p. 147; and *The Bach Reader*, p. 437 (whose translation I have altered slightly). Similar requirements for the Köthen *Stadtpfeifer* are documented in Herbert Zimpel, "In der Köthener Stadtpfeiferakte geblättert," *Cöthener Bach-Hefte* 3 (1985): 65–71.

[65] For the details of this interpretation and its social implications, see part 1.

the concertino, to a role completely overwhelming the full ensemble, and finally to one that, during the first section of the extended episode, in effect *becomes* the ensemble.[73]

The extraordinary length of the final episode (best labeled a *capriccio*[74] but nowadays still most often given the misnomer "cadenza"), being scored for unaccompanied harpsichord and featuring some rather extreme departures from the rhythmic and harmonic conventions of concerto style (see mm. 195–202), almost allows us on a first hearing to forget that the piece began as an ensemble work (we are typically unaware when listening to recordings that concert audiences, of course, see the flute and string players sitting there idly for the duration). Furthermore, Bach's handling of the mounting tension that is set up with the episode's prolonged pedal point, first by slowing down the rhythm from the thirty-seconds of m. 203 to the triplet sixteenths of m. 209, and then, moreover, by diffusing the harmonic tension of the dominant pedal through the A♯–B bass motion of mm. 213–14, may make the eventual V–I cadence marking the return of the ensemble for the closing ritornello seem less than entirely satisfying. Because the final ritornello does not serve directly to provide the long-awaited resolution of the A-major harpsichord pedal point, some listeners find it difficult to escape the sense that this ritornello thereby becomes somewhat ineffectual, perhaps positioned merely as a (stylistically desiderated) closing marker. Although the larger group does have the last word, so to speak, Bach's conventional closure by the ritornello, even with the affective strength of the *stile concitato*, may not have the power straightforwardly to succeed in containing the disruptiveness (musical and social) of the solo harpsichord material.[75]

---

[73] Bach even notates the harpsichord in the margrave's dedication score with a larger rastrum than for the other instruments. He may have done so more for visual effect than for the practical purpose of making the lines easier to read in performing situations. In the various eighteenth-century manuscript materials for this concerto, including those associated with the Bach family (see Besseler, *NBA* 7.2, Kritischer Bericht, pp. 101–10), the harpsichord, like each of the other instruments, is provided with its own separate performance part (i.e., the harpsichord player would not naturally expect to perform from a score, and the copyists of separate performing parts would not necessarily need the keyboard line in this score to be larger than the other parts).

[74] See Philip Whitmore, "Towards an Understanding of the Capriccio," *Journal of the Royal Musical Association* 113 (1988): 47–56; and *Unpremeditated Art: The Cadenza in the Classical Keyboard Concerto* (Oxford: Clarendon Press, 1991).

[75] Closing the fast movements with a tutti ritornello is something that, according to McClary's recent survey of the genre formulated compellingly in terms of social theory,

It is worth pointing out that a still little-known early version of this concerto has also survived. The entire piece was first published in 1975 as BWV 1050a in a supplement to Besseler's 1956 volume 7, part 2, of the *Neue Bach-Ausgabe*.[76] The most substantial differences between the versions are found in the *capriccio* for solo harpsichord, which is about three and a half times shorter in the BWV 1050a version.[77] This shorter episode more or less corresponds to the toccata-like mm. 197–214 of the Brandenburg version, before it cadences directly into the final ritornello. According to current research on Bach's procedures in revising his earlier works, Bach, hoping to make a greater impression on the margrave of Brandenburg, decided to clarify his concerto structure by expanding the original harpsichord solo with thematic references to the material from the main body of the movement (see mm. 154–95 in BWV 1050) before closing this longer episode with a refinement of whatever could be salvaged from the original episode (see mm. 197–213).[78]

Yet, even though the harpsichord episode is harmonically and formally more irregular in the BWV 1050a version than in BWV 1050, the final ritornello seems only in this earlier version to be straightforwardly successful in containing the disruptiveness of the solo harpsichord material. In BWV 1050a the rhythm of the pedal point does not become less active, and the harpsichord does not preempt the resolution of the mounting harmonic tension by coordinating an alteration to the pedal point with a move to a deceptive cadence. The closing ritornello functions directly as the harmonic resolution to the episode, and, therefore, the return of the ensemble does have a forceful effect (all the more so, considering that the pedal-point material

conventionally occurs in concertos to allow the group to contain any excesses from the soloists and thereby demonstrate that individual expression and social harmony are not incompatible (see "The Blasphemy of Talking Politics," p. 24).

[76] See n. 1. On the chronology of the various versions to the concerto, see Alfred Dürr, "Zur Entstehungsgeschichte des 5. Brandenburgischen Konzerts," *Bach-Jahrbuch* 61 (1975): 63–69.

[77] This early version has been recorded (Decca/L'Oiseau-Lyre 414 187 [London, 1985]) on period instruments by the Academy of Ancient Music with Christopher Hogwood, who suggests that BWV 1050a is musically much superior to the Brandenburg version. Hogwood's views are analyzed as an example of "the ultimate perversion of the idea of authenticity" by Richard Taruskin, "The Pastness of the Present and the Presence of the Past," in *Authenticity and Early Music: A Symposium*, ed. Nicholas Kenyon (Oxford: Oxford University Press, 1988), pp. 137–210, at pp. 192–93.

[78] George Stauffer, "Bach as Reviser of His Own Keyboard Works," *Early Music* 13 (1985): 185–98, at pp. 193–95.

inclines toward D minor and that, in featuring none of the harpsi-
chord-as-orchestra material of the later version [mm. 154–94], the
episode is relatively short).

The significance of Bach's substantial revisions to BWV 1050a may
lie less in his improving large-scale and small-scale compositional details of the concerto movement per se than in his giving a stronger
sense to an intensification pattern within the series of the six Brandenburg Concertos. Improvements in technical features emerge virtually inevitably even when Bach is merely making a neat copy of an
earlier work. Or, to make an observation referring more explicitly to
the composer's possible intentions, we may note that Bach's removing
certain compositional infelicities might in some cases be a side effect
of rather than the primary cause for revising a work. In BWV 1050a
the harpsichord ends up in the same sort of impasse that could be
seen in the struggle of the Fourth Brandenburg Concerto; in both
cases, we could unproblematically conclude that "all was well that
ended well." The progression described earlier, in which intensified
depiction of *concertare* in its primary meaning is coordinated with
greater chromaticism in the sense of the *Genera*, may be seen to have
been brought a significant step further with the BWV 1050 version of
the concerto.[79] In the first movement of the Fifth Brandenburg Concerto, was all really well, and did it really end well? This remarkable,
unprecedented (and unemulated) work appears to take one of the
two "concerto" notions to its very limits.[80]

[79] Bach possibly continued to perform the BWV 1050a version in Leipzig. Dürr established that the only surviving manuscript for this version (Mus. ms. Bach St 132,
Staatsbibliothek zu Berlin), is primarily in the hand of Johann Christoph Altnickol,
Bach's son-in-law, who copied out the concerto sometime between 1744 and 1759. Dürr
reports further that it is impossible to tell whether the exemplar for Altnickol's set of
parts was another set of parts or a score ("Zur Entstehungsgeschichte des 5. Brandenburgischen Konzerts," and *Nachtrag* to *NBA* 7.2). A close examination of St 132 in
the original reveals, however, that they were based on a set of parts: there are no corrected or uncorrected readings from adjacent lines in a score, and there are several
corrections of readings from close-by spots in the same line. (E.g., in Altnickol's violone
part at m. 41 of the first movement there is still faintly visible beneath the correct
reading an erasure of the violone's mm. 54–58a; interestingly, there are line breaks at
mm. 41 and 54 in Altnickol's violone part.) The apparent availability of a set of parts to
BWV 1050a in Leipzig raises the possibility that this version of the concerto was performed there.

[80] Bach's less well known, Leipzig concertos for solo harpsichord and ensemble
(BWV 1052–59) are in a different category (i.e., are less radical), perhaps partly because
they were all arranged from violin or oboe concertos, where the harpsichord is treated
rather differently from in the first movement of the Fifth Brandenburg Concerto.

Whether Bach's six concertos fall into patterns of pieces whose surface styles become more consortlike or more contentious, the outcome is in one significant respect more or less the same: both the most chromatic and the most enharmonic Brandenburg Concertos present the strongest abnegations of conventional scorings and attendant social associations.

IT MAY SEEM curious that Bach's symmetry in the tonal scheme, which, as we have seen, highlights the two notions of concerto, does not line up with the symmetry in the categories of scoring, which, as we have seen, highlights various applications of fortspinnung-type syntax. But the fact that the symmetries do not correspond should not be viewed as a flaw in the organization of the collection. Their systematically being out of phase could compel us to focus our attention separately on general aspects of concerto style that we might uncritically assume belong together. We are encouraged to see external categories (ensemble scoring versus soloistic scoring) as one matter and inner dynamics (*conserere* versus *concertare*) as another, the two things being certainly related but not necessarily connatural.[81]

[81] Separation of external and internal aspects by means of a discrepancy between tonal and formal schemes can also be found elsewhere in Bach. For example, in the cantata *Gottes Zeit ist die allerbeste Zeit* (BWV 106), Bach sets up an architectural symmetry of movement types (chorus-arioso-aria-chorus-aria-arioso-chorus) that does not line up with a symmetrical tonal plan (E♭–c–f–b♭–A♭–c–E♭—i.e., symmetrical in terms of key-signature levels). The structural center highlights the objective, doctrinal element of Christian faith expressed by the choral fugue ("Es ist der alte Bund"), whereas the tonal center points to the subjective, individual side of faith expressed by the following continuo aria ("In deine Hände befehl ich meinen Geist"). This interpretation of *Gottes Zeit* appears in Chafe, "Allegorical Music," p. 345, n. 11. A more detailed version appears in Chafe, *Tonal Allegory*, chap. 4.

CHAPTER THREE

Lutheran Belief and
Bach's Music

IT MIGHT be assumed that, by interpreting Bach's music socially, I have been picturing Bach as some sort of subversive or revolutionary. I am concerned here, therefore, to show that social interpretation of Bach's music is more properly understood and best accounted for in the wider context of his theological background.[1] The social views in Bach's Lutheranism fundamentally have very little or nothing to do with subversive or revolutionary thought.

Luther writes about social structure in many places, but perhaps the clearest and strongest expression of his ideas appears in his lectures on the book of Deuteronomy:

> Should justice and love not be observed also toward a stranger? The answer is that this, too, is according to a just principle of public order, that by some privilege citizens are honored beyond outsiders and strangers, lest everything be uniform and equal. . . . The world has need of these forms, even if they appear to have a show of inequality, like the status of servants and maids or workmen and laborers. For not all can be kings, princes, senators, rich men, and freemen in the same manner, since the world cannot exist without persons of various and different sorts. While before God there is no respect of persons (Acts 10.34), but all are equal, yet in the world respect of persons and inequality is necessary. And the purpose of this is that evildoers be curbed and the public peace stand firm, which it cannot do when persons are equal and without distinction.[2]

---

[1] A slightly different version of this discussion has appeared in "J. S. Bach's Brandenburg Concertos as a Meaningful Set," *Musical Quarterly* 77 (1993): 193–235.

[2] Martin Luther, *Lectures on Deuteronomy*, trans. Richard R. Caemmerer, ed. Jaroslav Pelikan, in *Luther's Works* (St. Louis: Concordia, 1960), vol. 9, p. 145. Luther presents the same thoughts in a less concentrated form in his long commentary on Psalm 111—nowadays this is probably the best-known of Luther's discussions, for it figures prominently in Max Weber, *The Protestant Ethic and the Spirit of Capitalism*, trans. Talcott Par-

Luther believed that the social hierarchy served a useful purpose and ought to be accepted. This hierarchy does not carry the highest significance, however, for it has to do only with worldly appearance and has no bearing on ultimate questions concerning faith, justification, and salvation.[3]

There are some intriguing indications beyond those gathered from his music that Bach considered the figuration of his orchestra in terms similar to Luther's social hierarchy. (Of course, as mentioned earlier,[4] Bach's orchestra does not have to be understood as a direct representation of contemporary society; rather, early eighteenth-century orchestral and social structures should be seen as products of certain modes of hierarchical thinking.) These indications are found in the Luther Commentary-Bible surviving from Bach's personal library. Bach's Bible is an especially interesting document, for it features not only interspersed commentary provided by the seventeenth-century Lutheran theologian Abraham Calov but also a considerable

---

sons (New York: Scribner's, 1958), p. 215. There were various oral or written sources from which Bach could have become acquainted with these ideas. That he was familiar with them is attested by the first recitatives from his church cantatas *Nur jedem das Seine*, BWV 163, and *Tue Rechnung! Donnerwort*, BWV 168 (cf. the final recitative from *Du Friedefürst, Herr Jesu Christ*, BWV 116). In any event, Luther's Commentary on Psalm 111 was printed in at least three of the books found in Bach's extensive personal library of theological works (see Robin A. Leaver, *Bachs Theologische Bibliothek: Eine kritische Bibliographie* [Neuhaussen-Stuttgart: Hänssler, 1983]): vol. 5 of the Jena edition of Luther's works (various printings; see Kurt Aland, *Hilfsbuch zum Lutherstudium*, rev. ed. [Witten: Luther-Verlag, 1970], p. 578), vol. 3 of the Wittenberg edition (Aland, 554), and vol. 1, book 2, of Abraham Calov's edition of the Luther Bible with interspersed excerpts from Luther's commentaries (Wittenberg, 1682; Bach's exemplar is housed in Concordia Seminary Library, St. Louis). For similar ideas see also Luther, "On Secular Authority," in *Luther and Calvin on Secular Authority*, trans. and ed. Harro Höpfl (Cambridge: Cambridge University Press, 1991), pp. 8, 33, 39. This essay was printed in vol. 2 of Bach's Jena edition of Luther's works (Aland, 574) and in vol. 2 of the Altenburg edition (Aland, 598), which Bach acquired in the 1740s (Leaver, *Bachs Theologische Bibliothek*, pp. 42, 52–54).

[3] The classic, if partly controversial, discussion of the historical implications of Luther's social views is chap. 3 of Weber, *The Protestant Ethic*. Weber was concerned to show that Lutheranism with its essential ambivalence toward the world was not well suited for the development of the spirit of capitalism, whereas Calvinism with its more worldly ideology was suited perfectly: in Calvinism the pursuit of wealth as an end in itself was still reprehensible, but its attainment as a fruit of labor in a calling was a sign of God's blessing, an indication of belonging to the elect (those predestined through God's grace for salvation)—that is, unlike in Roman Catholicism, good works could not help people to secure places in heaven.

[4] See n. 10 in the introduction.

number of marginal comments and underlinings that have been identified as coming from Bach's pen.[5] The most relevant excerpt for the
present purposes comes from the opening of the twenty-fifth (mis-
printed as twenty-sixth) chapter of 1 Chronicles, a passage partly un-
derlined by Bach and further highlighted by his marginal comment,
"N.B.: this chapter is the true foundation of all God-pleasing church
music. *And so on*" (emphasis mine):

> The singers and instrumentalists.
>
> [Text in parentheses is Calov's commentary and appears that
> way—with smaller print—in Bach's Bible.] v.1. And David set
> apart from the captains for service among the children of Asaph,
> Heman, and Jeduthun, the prophets (who were to form God's
> word in spiritual hymns and psalms and sing them in the temple,
> at the same time playing instruments) with harps, psalteries, and
> cymbals and they were numbered (and arranged in order) for
> work by their office (to place the matter in a certain order [das-
> selbe in gewisser Ordnung zu verrichten]. For God is a God of
> order. 1 Corinthians 14.33).[6]

Notice the resonance the end of Calov's commentary has with the
excerpt from Luther's lecture on Deuteronomy: both link hierarchy
with order. This connection is worth exploring further through an
examination of the next passage that was highlighted by Bach, 1
Chronicles 28.21 and its commentary, especially because it is also
marked by Bach's marginal comment "N.B. A splendid proof that besides other arrangements [Anstalten] of the service of worship, music
too was especially ordered [angeordnet] by God's spirit through
David":

> v. 21. Behold the hierarchy [Ordnung] of the priests and Levites
> for all the services in the house of God, they are with you in all
> the work and are willing and able for all services as are the

---

[5] For bibliographical information on the Calov Bible, see n. 2. Scientific research has
determined that the chemical content of the ink in the underlinings is the same as that
of the marginal comments whose handwriting characteristics were identified with
Bach's by Hans-Joachim Schulze (Bach-Archiv, Leipzig); see Bruce Kusko, "Proton
Milloprobe Analysis of the Hand-Penned Annotations in Bach's Calov Bible," in
Howard H. Cox, ed., *The Calov Bible of J. S. Bach* (Ann Arbor: UMI Research Press, 1985),
pp. 31–106.

[6] This translation is found in Cox, *The Calov Bible*, p. 418.

princes and the people for all your dealings. (which you will grasp. It is clear however from this divine model and from all prophetic direction of David that he has accomplished nothing through his own works, in the building and management of the temple and the worship service but rather through the model that the Lord has placed before him by his spirit, in every respect and according to the dealings of service in whatever manner God has placed them in his heart. For one serves God in vain with willful or selfish services. Matthew 15.9. God prescribes, carves out, calculates, and arranges everything for us and thus explains his will how he wants to be respected by us; therefore in matters of religion we should presume and do nothing without his revealed word. Take this as a warning against human action and self-ordained worship and law-giving. For example, against the audacity and presumption of the pope who sets himself above the scripture.)[7]

Bach's marginal comment allows (perhaps intentionally) for both meanings of the word *anordnen*, an ambiguity retained in the translation by the word *order*. *Anordnen* means both "to give a command (or 'order')" and "to put into order (e.g., a hierarchy)." The latter understanding involves an extension of a formerly purely military term: "to put troops in their proper order for an attack"; the widening of meaning occurred in the second half of the seventeenth century.[8] In addition, the word *Anstalt*, as Bach uses it here, may have richer meanings than can be easily captured in translation. *Anstalt* arose in the seventeenth-century chanceries as "measure," "disposition," "order."[9]

Bach seems to be saying not merely that God wants there to be music in service of the church but also that musical hierarchies are part of the God-ordained order of things in this world. The musicians referred to in Chronicles were a division of the Levites, and they were thus "ordained" in their office.[10] The Levites figured lower in the hier-

---

[7] Ibid.

[8] See Keith Spalding, *An Historical Dictionary of German Figurative Usage* (Oxford: Blackwell, [1952]–), vol. 1, p. 54.

[9] Ibid., p. 62.

[10] See Robin Leaver, *J. S. Bach and Scripture: Glosses from the Calov Bible Commentary* (St. Louis: Concordia, 1985), pp. 95–96. Incidentally, although in theory orthodox Lutheran theologians considered music in the worship service as among the *adiaphora*

archy of the temple's strict, class-conscious organization than the priests; the priests were thus the ones, for example, who took on the relatively prestigious task of playing trumpets, whereas all other musical performance was assigned to Levites.[11]

In short, then, the aim of these social interpretations of Bach's music is not to show that Bach advocated or foresaw revolutionary action against contemporary social hierarchies but rather to suggest that he may be telling or reminding his listeners of the significant Lutheran viewpoint that such figurations have only to do with the present world and therefore are without ultimate significance.[12]

It should perhaps be emphasized that Bach's concertos were designed not for posterity but for eighteenth-century audiences made up mostly of fellow Lutherans. Within a Lutheran milieu there would be no reason to find a necessary contradiction between the conservative social views expressed in Bach's Bible notations and the hierarchy-questioning aspects of the scorings and forms in his concertos. In this context there would be no need for a theological veto against progressive political action to be expressed clearly within the music

---

(things indifferent), in paractice they considered it to be essential; see Joyce Irwin, "Music and the Doctrine of Adiaphora in Orthodox Lutheran Theology," *The Sixteenth Century Journal* 14 (1983): 157–72; cited in Leaver, *J. S. Bach and Scripture*, p. 96.

[11] See Howard H. Cox, "Bach's Conception of His Office," *Bach* (the journal of the Riemenschneider Bach Institute) 20, no. 1 (1989): 22–30, at p. 28. Bach highlighted a passage from 2 Chronicles 5.12–13 describing the priests playing trumpets and the Levites playing other instruments and singing praise to God, who then appears in the form of a cloud. Bach added the marginal comment "N.B.: with a devotional [andächtigen] music God is always present with his grace"; trans. in Cox, *The Calov Bible*, p. 419; see also Leaver, *J. S. Bach and Scripture*, pp. 97–98.

[12] In discussing Bach's study of the Calov Bible, I do not mean to suggest that there was some sort of causal connection between his highlighting various Lutheran commentaries and his composing the Brandenburg Concertos. For one thing, we do not know when Bach obtained this Bible (his monogrammed signature with date "1733" in the flyleaves notwithstanding—see Gerhard Herz, "J. S. Bach 1733: A 'New' Bach Signature," in *Studies in Renaissance and Baroque Music in Honor of Arthur Mendel*, ed. Robert L. Marshall [Kassel: Bärenreiter, 1974], pp. 255–63); and for another thing, we do not know in many cases when Bach's underlinings and marginalia were entered. My view is that both Bach's concertos and his marginal comments reflect his ongoing interest in certain basic social issues. In seeing a continuity between Bach's concertos and his reading of Chronicles, I do not wish, however, to give the impression that Bach had a static religious sensibility. The social views I have cited are fairly basic to Lutheran theology, and so far as I can tell are not likely to have changed essentially in Bach's mind.

in order for such a veto to come into operation. As part of their culture, Bach's immediate contemporaries understood that ever since the Fall of humanity into sin, it became necessary for hierarchies to be maintained in the present world. According to Lutherans, especially seventeenth- and eighteenth-century Lutherans, the true purpose of music, including instrumental music, even apart from its liturgical uses, was to glorify God and to uplift people spiritually by turning their minds to heavenly matters.[13] One important message of Lutheran theology, and, I am arguing, of Bach's concertos, was that in the next world, the heavenly one, the hierarchies of our present earthly world will no longer be necessary.[14] In other words, Bach's music more likely instructed its listeners how to think about and spiritually cope with contemporary hierarchies than how to act upon them.

Today we are free, of course, to bring new meanings to Bach's music. The task of hermeneutics, however, has for many centuries been understood to involve synthesizing historical interpretations of texts with modern concerns. Viewing Bach's music as politically progressive—overriding contexts that we may find contradictory—might, it seems to me, involve not reconciliation of historical and modern concerns but simple appropriation.[15]

Already in considering Bach's reading of the Calov commentary Bible, we get a fairly clear sense of his conservative stance toward the social structures of the present world. But Bach's conservatism is also evident, for example, from the way he handled himself in the continual troubles with his superiors. Significantly, nowhere in the surviving documents is there any hint of Bach's feeling that he ought to be

---

[13] On this point, see Irwin, "Music and the Doctrine of Adiaphora," pp. 157–72.

[14] Luther also clearly understood the verse from Luke quoted as the epigraph for this book in spiritual, not political, terms. See Martin Luther, *The Magnificat*, trans. A.T.W. Steinhaeuser, ed. Jaroslav Pelikan, in *Luther's Works* (St. Louis: Concordia, 1956), vol. 21, pp. 295–355. (Bach owned several copies of this commentary.)

[15] Compare Susan McClary, "The Blasphemy of Talking Politics during Bach Year," in *Music and Society: The Politics of Composition, Performance and Reception*, ed. Richard Leppert and Susan McClary (Cambridge: Cambridge University Press, 1987), pp. 13–62, at p. 61: "I would propose the age-old strategy of rewriting the tradition in such a way as to appropriate Bach to our own political ends." Compare also Theodor Adorno, "Bach Defended against His Devotees," in Adorno, *Prisms*, trans. Samuel Weber and Shierry Weber (1967; reprint, Cambridge, Mass.: M.I.T. Press, 1981), pp. 133–46.

appreciated and recognized for his talents rather than for his official position. In his various clashes, Bach does not question the validity of contemporary hierarchies but, in fact, continually invokes his place in the hierarchy as part of his defense.[16] Bach's arguments—whether they are correct or not does not affect the present point—are that others have improperly assumed the prerogatives that go with his station; it is quite remarkable how forcefully Bach focuses on the nature of his official positions (notice his repeated use of the words *Amt* and *Officio*). Although Bach certainly experienced many troubles with the authorities, there is no clear evidence that he had the continual "trouble with Authority" that is traditionally—though often unhistorically—associated with Western musical artists (a more plausible association since Mozart's, and especially Beethoven's, time). It may be significant, incidentally, that Bach's most protracted difficulties were with authorities who espoused Enlightenment ideas.[17]

Taking Bach's instrumental music solely by itself, we could find the meanings ambiguous (to what purpose do Bach's concertos question hierarchies?): the notes themselves do not clearly indicate whether the music's ideals are to be realized in the present or in the next world. This is why the contexts of Bach's Lutheranism, his vocal music, and verbal documents are also worth taking into consideration. They do not contradict what might be called a conservative interpretation of the Brandenburg Concertos. For a politically progressive reading of the concertos, it would be important specifically to show that the verbal documents and Bach's vocal music do not speak against such an interpretation.

[16] The relevant documents are conveniently brought together under the title "Der unbequeme Untergebene" (the unwieldy subordinate) in *Johann Sebastian Bach: Leben und Werk in Dokumenten*, ed. Hans-Joachim Schulze (Leipzig: VEB Deutscher Taschenbuch Verlag, 1975), pp. 40–58. Translations of nearly all these are found in Hans T. David and Arthur Mendel, eds., *The Bach Reader: A Life of Johann Sebastian Bach in Letters and Documents*, rev. ed. (New York: Norton, 1966); see pp. 51–53, 75, 98–105, 113–15, 119–24, 137–49. Consider, too, that the highest number of markings in Bach's Calov Bible is found in Ecclesiastes, a book that refers continually to accepting one's lot as being much more important than worldly recognition and to the notion that intelligent people are in for a life of suffering but nowhere that talent is inherently praiseworthy, above the demands of meeting one's official duties.

[17] Consider especially the almost painfully tedious dispute between Bach and Johann August Ernesti (rector at the Thomas-Schule in Leipzig) over the right to appoint prefects. See Schulze, *Johann Sebastian Bach: Leben und Werk in Dokumenten*, pp. 47–57; and David, *The Bach Reader*, pp. 137–49.

It might, on the other hand, be suggested that Bach's instrumental music simply has a different message from that of his vocal music— that his musical output has two different "voices," the one perhaps conscious (music with texts), and the other unconscious (instrumental music) and therefore more telling. I have argued from the various historical contexts that we do not encounter contradictory voices in Bach's musical output. A progressive interpretation would need to show either that all Bach's music is indeed progressive or that any multiplicity of voice in his output inherently and unavoidably involves contradiction (and, furthermore, that the progressive elements override the conservative ones).[18] Neither of these has, so far as I am aware, been tried. The former would be extremely difficult to do. As for the latter, a Freudian approach to what we might see as a conflict between Bach's documented religious views and his concertos— though intellectually appealing—does not, in my opinion, work. I think we have to see Bach the way the American literary scholar Harold Bloom sees Shakespeare: before (and, in any event, beyond) any such forms of "anxiety."[19] (All the same, it seems rather doubtful that Bach's remarkable handling of scorings and forms in his concertos could have been essentially unconscious.) Even more quickly than with most interpretive situations, it may here at a certain point come down to matters of belief and to how thoroughly and compellingly one reasons through them.

INTERPRETING the Brandenburg Concertos in terms of extramusical implications of relationships between the forms and the scorings has exposed a partly didactic character in Bach's court-entertainment music—that is, in works that have come to be considered "pure" of the sorts of references confronted in his more obviously applied music such as the cantatas written for the Lutheran liturgy. With their strong social implications, the set of Brandenburg Concertos would effectively counter the view of Bach's contemporaries, advanced forcefully, for example, by Mattheson, that concertos "lacked moral

[18] A more extreme option would be to say that the meanings of Bach's music should not be controlled primarily, or at all, by its author or contexts. In that case, a progressive view could also quickly become untenable, for the notion that Bach's music has social significance of any sort also depends on invoking history.

[19] See Bloom, *The Anxiety of Influence: A Theory of Poetry* (London: Oxford University Press, 1973), p. 11.

and laudable purpose" when not connected with some specifically text-related situation (e.g., introducing an opera, or enhancing a church service).[20] Bach had, it seems, a much broader view of what would constitute "texts," and he had the requisite skill and imagination to produce instrumental music that referred to them.

[20] See Arthur Hutchings, *The Baroque Concerto*, rev. ed. [London: Faber, 1973], p. 175, quoting, without page reference, Johann Mattheson, *Der musicalische Patriot* (Hamburg, 1728). What Hutchings says seems to fit with the contents of at least this book of Mattheson's, but I have not succeeded in locating the quotation. Views of several contemporary writers questioning the value of concertos on account of their typically nonreferential character are discussed in Bellamy Hosler, *Changing Aesthetic Views of Instrumental Music in Eighteenth-Century Germany* (Ann Arbor: UMI Research Press, 1981).

Text-Critical Notes on
Early Copies of the
Sixth Brandenburg Concerto

I N H I S critical report for the *Neue Bach-Ausgabe*, Heinrich Besseler lists a number of readings that are common to the manuscripts Mus. ms. Bach St 150 and Mus. ms. Bach P 265 (both in the Staatsbibliothek zu Berlin) but that vary from the readings of the margrave's dedication score (Am.B.78, likewise Berlin). Besseler claims that P 265 was copied from St 150 and suggests that either the copyist of St 150 made "arbitrary additions" to the readings of Am.B.78 or based his copy on a now lost alternate, perhaps authentic, transmission of the concerto.[1]

Besseler gives the following reasons for concluding that P 265 was copied from St 150 (the first six are to establish the relationship of the two manuscripts to each other, whereas the last two are to establish the priority of St 150):[2]

In mm. 22–24, 37–39, 62–64, 96–100, and 107–9 of the gamba parts in the first movement, both manuscripts provide trills that are not found in Am.B.78.

N. 5 in m. 38 of the first gamba part is an e♮ in both manuscripts but an e♭ in Am.B.78.

N. 3 in m. 42 of the first viola part is an f′ in both manuscripts but a d′ in Am.B.78.

In mm. 40 and 59 of the second movement, the continuo part in both manuscripts has the indication "tasto," a marking not found in Am.B.78.

---

[1] Heinrich Besseler, ed., Johann Sebastian Bach, *Neue Ausgabe sämtlicher Werke* (*Neue Bach Ausgabe*), vol. 7, part 2: *Sechs Brandenburgische Konzerte*, Kritischer Bericht (Kassel: Bärenreiter, 1956), p. 143; compare Besseler's comments about additions to St 150 in Kritischer Bericht, p. 142, where he attributes some of the additions to Carl Friedrich Zelter, the director of the Berlin Singakademie in the early nineteenth century.

[2] Besseler, Kritischer Bericht, pp. 143–44.

N. 1 in m. 47 of the second viola part is an eighth-note grace in both manuscripts but a sixteenth-note grace in Am.B.78.

The continuo part is richly and identically figured for all three movements in both manuscripts but is unfigured in Am.B.78.

The last quarter of m. 16 of the cello part in the first movement reads as the two eighth notes f–F in P 265 but as an eighth and two sixteenths f–F–f in St 150 and Am.B.78.

N. 4 of m. 91 of the second viola part is a c′ in P 265 but an e♭′ in St 150 and Am.B.78.

THE VALIDITY of all but the last two of Besseler's observations may be questioned:

The additional trills in the first movement clearly were not added by the scribes of St 150 and P 265. In both cases the handwriting and the ink color of these entries is not the same as, for example, those for the trills that are common to St 150, P 265, and Am.B.78. Besseler does not mention that the supplementary trills do not appear in the part labeled "Viola da Gamba Prima" in St 150. They appear in the part labeled "Viola terza," which was arranged as a substitute for the "Viola da Gamba Prima" part.[3]

---

[3] The added indication "Anstatt der Viola da Gamba prima" is in the handwriting of Zelter. (This is mentioned by Besseler, Kritischer Bericht, p. 142.) The "Viola terza" part, notated in alto clef, has no text-critical value separate from St 150, for, as might be expected, the part was copied directly from the "Viola da Gamba Prima" part of St 150, notated in tenor clef. For example, n. 2 of m. 17 to n. 4 of m. 19 in the "Viola terza" part was originally copied a fifth too high. In the "Viola da Gamba Prima" part, mm. 33 and following appear in the same point in the line two staves lower. The copyist apparently skipped over two staves at the pickup to m. 18 (i.e., the readings of mm. 32–33 are the same as mm. 17–18, though a fifth higher), returned to the correct place by m. 19 (i.e., m. 34 is slightly different from m. 19), and then discovered that he was transposing more than a third. This error is difficult to explain if the part were supposed to be copied from P 265, and there are in fact no indications in the part that it was copied from a score. Slight modifications were necessary in mm. 36, 95, and 96, where the gamba line goes below the range of the viola. These simple and straightforward changes were entered in red ink and in pencil on top of the original readings in P 265. The different colors suggest, but cannot prove, that these revisions in P 265 were copied from the "Viola terza" part (it would not be the other way around, for the reasons mentioned earlier), where the revisions are given without traces of Bach's original readings (St 150 and P 265 were both associated with Zelter and the Berlin Singakademie).

For n. 5 in m. 38 of the first gamba part the natural sign was added in both St 150 and P 265: in St 150 it is squeezed in as a revision in the "Viola da Gamba Prima" part and apparently added later to the "Viola terza" part, whereas in P 265 it is added by a quill of a different thickness and in slightly differently colored ink from the rest of the score.[4]

N. 3 in m. 42 of the first viola part is an f′ only in St 150. Am.B.78 and P 265 both give d′.[5]

The indication "tasto" in mm. 40 and 59 of the second movement of the continuo part in both manuscripts is not found in Am.B.78, but these indications were added to St 150 and P 265 in a lighter ink in all four cases.

N. 1 in m. 47 of the second viola part is an eighth-note grace only in St 150, where it appears without a slur. In Am.B.78 and P 265 it is a sixteenth-note grace with a slur.

The continuo figures in St 150 and P 265 were added in a different ink color.

THERE ARE a number of obvious reasons why P 265 could not have been copied from St 150. First, the following uncorrected errors appear in St 150, readings not transmitted in P 265:[6]

N. 3 in m. 42 of the first viola part in the first movement is an f′ in St 150, while P 265 gives d′, the correct reading.

N. 1 in m. 83 of the second viola part is a c′ in St 150, whereas P 265 gives an a, which is the correct reading.

Second, the following corrected errors in P 265 indicate that the copyist was working from a score, not a set of parts:

---

[4] This was apparently the Singakademie solution to an infelicitous e♭ in their exemplar. Am.B.78 gives e♮ here, which may be explained as a transposition error from the note g in Bach's alto-clef exemplar (for details on this, see appendix 2).

[5] If Besseler had reported the state of affairs for m. 42 accurately in his discussion "Zur Abhängigkeit der Quellen" (Kritischer Bericht, pp. 143–44), he would have been forced to admit that P 265 could not have been copied from St 150. Ironically, without a check of the manuscripts, the correctly reported information under "Takt 42" in his discussion "Spezielle Anmerkungen" (ibid., p. 146) would easily be interpreted as a typographical error (i.e., the Neue Bach-Ausgabe would have forgotten to type ", D" here).

[6] For another reason that P 265 is unlikely to have been copied from St 150, see the comments on m. 47 of the second movement (these are found three paragraphs above in the main text).

Nn. 5–6 in m. 42 of the first gamba part in the first movement were originally entered a step higher. In this measure, nn. 2–4 of the second viola part occupy the same positions on the staff as nn. 2–4 of the first gamba part (d' in alto clef corresponds to b in tenor clef[7]). The copyist accidentally switched to the viola line (up one staff in a score) and did not notice his error until he arrived at n. 7.

Nn. 7–8 in m. 47 of the second gamba part were originally entered a fourth lower. In this measure, all the notes of the cello part occupy the same positions on the staff as those of the second gamba part (c in bass clef corresponds to g in tenor clef). The copyist accidentally switched to the cello line (down one staff in a score) and did not notice his error until he arrived at m. 48 or 49.

N. 12 in m. 27 of the second viola part in the third movement was originally entered a sixth higher. In this measure the viola parts play in unison for nn. 1–11. The copyist accidentally switched to the first viola line (up one staff in a score) and did not notice his error until he arrived at m. 28.

N. 3 in m. 45 of the cello part was originally entered a third lower. It is possible that for one note the copyist accidentally switched to the second gamba line (up one staff in a score).

Third, the following indications in P 265 suggest that it is dependent on Am.B.78:[8]

N. 3 in m. 58 of the first gamba part in the first movement reads e♭ instead of f. Bach placed this note very low in Am.B.78, and therefore it could easily be misread.

Nn. 1–4 in m. 87 of the first gamba part are beamed in two groups of two instead of one group of four. In Am.B.78 Bach beamed

---

[7] This point is labored here because it might be easy to forget that the manuscripts transmit the gamba parts in the tenor clef (the *Neue Bach-Ausgabe* prints them in alto clef).

[8] These indications point to either a direct or an indirect dependence of P 265 on Am.B.78. The only indication of a possible direct dependence is found in m. 37 of the third movement. At this point in Am.B.78, there is a conspicuous *X*, something that may have been put there for tracking purposes by the copyist of P 265 at the end of one of his copying sessions, for m. 37 marks a page turn from fol. 9ʳ to 9ᵛ in P 265. (So far as the present discussion is concerned, however, it would not matter whether the dependence is direct or indirect.)

the notes that way in order to make room for the low notes of the second viola part in the first half of the measure.

Nn. 1–8 in m. 107 of the first viola part were originally entered a third too low. In Am.B.78 Bach notated mm. 107 and 108 of the first viola part with contiguous ledger lines, and therefore they could easily be misread.

N. 6 in m. 38 of the cello part in the second movement reads e♭ instead of f. In Am.B.78 there is an inkblot directly above nn. 3–6 of this measure, and therefore n. 6 could easily be misread. A copyist might not notice that Bach placed a clarifying tablature letter above the note.

N. 5 in m. 39 to n. 1 in m. 40 of the first viola part are tied, whereas nn. 1–2 in m. 40 are not slurred. In Am.B.78 Bach notated the slur for nn. 1–2 in m. 40 somewhat carelessly to the left, and therefore it could be misread as a tie.

N. 3 in m. 30 of the cello part in the third movement has a flat sign instead of a natural sign. In Am.B.78 the bottom half of the natural sign is contiguous with the slur, and therefore it could be misread as a flat sign.

Nn. 11–18 in m. 54 of the first viola part originally read differently (the reading beneath the erasure here is illegible). In Am.B.78 Bach notated the ledger lines contiguously, and therefore the notes could originally have been misread.

CURIOUSLY, after stating that the copyist of P 265 used St 150 as his exemplar,[9] Besseler mentions that the copyist possibly in the meantime had taken a look at Am.B.78 or Am.B.77 (an apograph copy of Am.B.78, now found in the Staatsbibliothek zu Berlin), something suggested by peculiarities in one spot in P 265.[10] Besseler goes on to say (accurately) that in m. 41 of the first viola part in the second movement Am.B.78 and the manuscripts Am.B.77 and P 265 provide unnecessary flat signs for nn. 4 and 6, whereas n. 5, obviously requiring a flat sign, has no accidental. Besseler then claims that St 150 gives the flat for n. 5 but not for nn. 4 and 6. There are, however, no accidentals at all for this measure in St 150. It is strange that Besseler should have fabricated an accidental for n. 5 in St 150, for it (needlessly) under-

[9] Kritischer Bericht, p. 143.
[10] Ibid., p. 144.

mines his suggestion that P 265 was copied from St 150: if P 265 had been copied from St 150 and then had "possibly in the meantime" been compared by the copyist to Am.B.78, P 265 would have accidentals for all three notes. Perhaps the potential advantage for Besseler of the claim lies in the fact that it provides a (rather backhanded) way of adducing evidence for the independence of St 150 after all from Am.B.78. (Cf. the Kritischer Bericht, p. 143: "If the copyist of St 150 actually used Am.B.77 or Am.B.78 as his exemplar, then he brought forth many independent additions, including arbitrary ones. It would even be conceivable that St 150 was based on another copy or entirely on an authentic earlier version than the one we know from Bach's score for the margrave of Brandenburg."). The reason it would be advantageous to Besseler if there were evidence for even an only slightly different version of the Sixth Brandenburg Concerto is that if St 150 and P 265 were dependent on Am.B.78, there would be available no (text-critical) evidence against the potential suggestion that the Sixth Brandenburg Concerto was among the last of the set to be composed. That suggestion would threaten the teleological interpretation in Besseler's important article on the development of Bach's concerto style.[11]

THE FOLLOWING indications suggest that St 150 was copied from a score, and of these, the last three support, although not overwhelmingly, the notion that St 150 was copied from Am.B.78:

M. 44 of the cello part in the second movement was originally entered an octave lower. The copyist accidentally switched to the continuo line (one staff lower in a score) and did not notice his error until m. 45.

N. 8 in m. 16 of the second gamba part in the first movement appears originally to have been entered a sixth higher (it is not fully clear whether there is an erasure here). The copyist may have accidentally switched to the first gamba line (one staff higher in a score).

Nn. 1–4 in m. 34 of the first gamba part originally read c′–a–b♭–c′, that is, the reading of nn. 1–4 in m. 35 of the second gamba

[11] Besseler, "Zur Chronologie der Konzerte Joh. Seb. Bachs," in *Festschrift Max Schneider zum achtzigsten Geburtstag*, ed. Walther Vetter (Leipzig: VEB Deutscher Verlag für Musik, 1955), pp. 115–28.

part. The copyist accidentally switched down one staff in a score and did not notice his error until the second half of m. 35. The error was easy to fall into, because mm. 33–34 in the first gamba part equal mm. 34–35 in the second gamba part (and, presumably, because m. 33 marks a page break in Am.B.78).

N. 8 in m. 52 of the first viola part is very thick and perhaps partly erased. Bach placed this note, c′, somewhat low in Am.B.78, and that might explain why the copyist of St 150 appears originally to have entered this note as a b♭.

N. 4 in m. 56 of the cello part was originally entered a twelfth lower. Bach placed an f here between the cello and continuo lines in Am.B.78, and because of the way he wrote the f and notated the stem for n. 4 (an a), it is remotely possible, in a serious lapse of attention, to read this as a note D. The copyist of St 150 must have immediately switched down one staff to the continuo line, for there is an erased bar line after n. 4 (i.e., the last note of the measure in the continuo line is a D).

IT IS BY NOW clear that St 150 and P 265 offer no readings of Bach's independent from those of Am.B.78. Interestingly (in light of Besseler's presentation), the only indications of different readings from the Am.B.78 transmission are to be found in the dedication score itself:

In mm. 17–18, the first half of m. 19, and first half of m. 32 of the continuo part in the first movement, the continuous eighth notes originally were entered as quarter notes with quarter-note rests.[12]

[12] These revisions are mentioned neither in Besseler's Kritischer Bericht nor in Peter Wackernagel, "Beobachten am Autograph von Bachs Brandenburgischen Konzerten," in *Festschrift Max Schneider*, pp. 129–38.

Notes on Bach's Notation of the Gamba Parts in the Margrave of Brandenburg's Dedication Score

IN HIS article for *Die Musikforschung* on the Brandenburg Concertos,[1] Martin Geck suggests that Bach based the Sixth Brandenburg Concerto on a trio sonata composed early in his career and scored for two violas or violin and viola and continuo. Geck makes the following observations to support his suggestion:

> The Sixth Brandenburg Concerto shows none of the modern stylistic traits of the Vivaldian concerto. Its old-fashioned style and scoring point to the Italian trio sonata. The gambas do not play in the second movement. They have only a continuo function in the third. And where they do play significant material in the first movement, the cello and continuo are usually silent.

> "Conspicuous parallel fifths" show up in the opening movement in the gamba parts in m. 22 and analogous points thereafter, right at places where the cello and continuo are silent. The fifths may well have emerged, unnoticed by Bach, as a result of the process of his reorchestrating an earlier piece. Considering the egregious and therefore obviously "unintentional" fifths that Bach entered as compositional revisions in the margrave's score of the Fifth Brandenburg Concerto,[2] one would have to conclude that Bach unintentionally allowed the errors to stand in the Sixth Concerto.

> The first viola part does not go below g in the second movement, and there is a correction from treble to alto clef in the last

---

[1] Geck, "Gattungstraditionen und Altersschichten in den Brandenburgischen Konzerten," *Die Musikforschung* 23 (1970): 139–52.

[2] See m. 11 and the subsequent analogous points in the first movement, where there are six parallel fifths in a row between the viola and the right hand of the harpsichord. (These readings are, altogether reasonably, not reproduced in modern editions.)

system of the third movement. This suggests a possible earlier scoring for violin on the top line of the concerto.

The gamba staves are empty for the second movement. Bach appears to have planned very carefully the ruling of staves in the margrave's score. Geck observes, for example, that Bach's numbers of staves in the scores for the first five concertos correspond exactly in each of the movements to the various scorings. Geck also observes, for example, that the way Bach arranged the large staff for the harpsichord part and the smaller staves for the other parts of the Fifth Concerto accommodates exactly the requirements of the first movement with its originally shorter harpsichord "cadenza."[3] Bach must have decided at the last minute to create a harpsichord solo three times as long, for he entered the longer episode into all the staves in the margrave's score, not only the large staff. It would not have been impractical to enter the much shorter episode into only the larger staff for the harpsichord. By analogy, it is possible that for the Sixth Brandenburg Concerto, Bach may not have decided until the last minute that the gambas would not play in the slow movement.

When one considers Bach's unusual treatment, musical and notational, of the gamba parts, it can hardly seem coincidental that the concentration of corrections in this concerto are in the gamba parts.

EACH OF Geck's observations can be questioned:

I explored, earlier in this book, an interpretation of the Sixth Brandenburg Concerto as an example of (unconventional) Vivaldi reception in Bach. The unusual treatment of the gambas was interpreted not as a defect (i.e., pointing to an earlier version without gambas) but as an integral aspect of the meaning (and therefore probably also, although not necessarily, of the original design) of the piece. If there were an earlier scoring, this would not invalidate the interpretation of the piece in the form that we know it.

[3] This had been pointed out in Christoph Wolff, "Die Rastrierungen in den Original-handschriften Johann Sebastian Bachs und ihre Bedeutung für die diplomatische Quellenkritik," in *Festschrift für Friedrich Smend zum 70. Geburtstag* (Berlin: Merseburger, 1963), pp. 80–92.

The comparison of the direct fifths in m. 22 and analogous places in the first movement with the parallel fifths in m. 11 of the Fifth Brandenburg Concerto is not apt. The direct fifths in the Sixth Concerto do not mark changes of harmony, and therefore they do not constitute contrapuntal errors.

Because there are no visible revisions in the first viola part in the margrave's score, it is unlikely that Bach arranged it there from a violin part (see especially the considerable number of places that the part goes below the range of the violin). Occasional corrections of the clef from treble to alto (see first movement, m. 33; second movement, m. 61; third movement, m. 63) might support Geck's hypothesis if there were also any compositional revisions pointing to an origin for violin. By themselves the clef corrections are not meaningful. Bach very often, apparently in lapses of attention, carelessly enters inappropriate treble clefs in the uppermost lines of his scores.[4]

Empty staves for the gamba parts in the slow movement do not necessarily imply that Bach decided only at the last minute to exclude the gambas. See, for example, the empty staves for the horn parts in the slow movement of the First Brandenburg Concerto (i.e., Geck's observation that Bach's number of staves in the scores for the first five concertos corresponds ex-

[4] For example, in the following places in the recorder parts in the "composing scores" or composing-score sections in Bach's manuscripts, Bach corrected careless treble-clef entries to French violin clef (on the characteristics of Bach's composing scores, as opposed to his scores copied or revised from earlier manuscripts, see Robert L. Marshall, *The Compositional Process of J. S. Bach: A Study of the Autograph Scores of the Vocal Works* [Princeton: Princeton University Press, 1972], vol. 1, pp. 3–30): mm. 1, 22, and 137 of the opening chorus in *Brich dem Hungrigen dein Brot*, BWV 39; mm. 29, 55, 60, 74, and 88 of the opening chorus in *Herr Christ, der einge Gottessohn*, BWV 96; mm. 1, 27, 49, and 55 of the opening chorus in *Ihr werdet weinen und heulen*, BWV 103; mm. 5 and 30 of the opening chorus and m. 14 of the soprano aria in *Herr Jesu Christ, wahr' Mensch und Gott*, BWV 127; mm. 4, 27, and 42 of the alto aria in *Er rufet seinen Schafen mit Namen*, BWV 175; mm. 75 and 89 of the closing chorus in *Himmelskönig, sei willkommen*, BWV 182; and m. 21 of the alto aria in the *Magnificat*, BWV 243a. The same problem comes up in Bach's fair or revision copies of instrumental works with recorder, works for which there is no reason to believe that the originals were not conceived for recorder. For example, mm. 8, 48, and 88 in the first movement, m. 15 in the second movement, and m. 123 in the third movement of the Second Brandenburg Concerto; m. 109 in the first movement and m. 44 in the second movement of the Fourth Brandenburg Concerto; and mm. 66 and 186 in the first movement, m. 31 in the second movement, and m. 132 in the third movement of the Concerto in F major, BWV 1057.

actly to the scorings in each of the movements is erroneous). We know that Bach did not decide to exclude the horns at the last minute, because the eighteenth-century copy with the early scoring of the concerto (Mus. ms. Bach P 1061, Staatsbibliothek zu Berlin) also has no horns playing in the slow movement. It is possible, but of course unprovable, that Bach left the gamba staves empty in the Sixth Brandenburg Concerto for visual effect (recall the large harpsichord staff in the Fifth concerto and the atypical placing of the violin staff in the Fourth Concerto): the conventionally privileged gambas would not be merely absent from the score; they would be, as it were, conspicuously absent.

It is true that the concentration of changes is found in the gamba parts, but it is worth considering more closely what kind of changes they are. In fact Bach's score contains no compositional revisions, only corrections of copying errors from a third lower.[5] This suggests, as mentioned in the main text, that his exemplar was notated in alto clefs and that he may have transposed the parts to tenor clef for the visual effect of more strongly marking the separation of the gambas from the violas. It should be emphasized that the lack of compositional revisions in the gamba parts implies that the exemplar was also scored with gambas (i.e., not without the parts altogether, and not for some other instruments notated in alto clef). In the following places there are corrections from a third lower: n. 6 in m. 89, n. 3 in m. 92 (notice that the stem points the wrong way), and n. 1 in m. 99 through n. 3 in m. 100 (notice that for nn. 2–4 in m. 99 the stems point the wrong way) of the first movement in the second gamba part; similar corrections appear at n. 1 in m. 110 of the first movement and n. 1 in m. 45 of the third movement in the first gamba part. At m. 17 of the first movement in the first gamba part, there are two custodes, one of them a third too low. In m. 38 of the first movement in the first gamba part, the fifth note is an obviously incorrect e♭.

---

[5] The only other kind of copying error is found in mm. 5 and 6 of the first gamba part. The first four notes of m. 5 were originally a step lower, whereas the last four notes of m. 5 and the first four notes of m. 6 were originally a step higher. Bach had apparently reverted to "automatic pilot" with the pattern of mm. 1–4.

In alto clef this would read as the correct note, g, and therefore the e♭ can be viewed as an uncorrected transposition error from alto clef.[6] In m. 89 of the first movement in the first and second gamba parts Bach originally entered bass clefs. Bach could very easily have shifted down two staves in his exemplar if the upper four parts were notated there in alto clef.

[6] Modern editions correct the note to read g. The early copies of the piece, discussed in appendix 1, altered the note by adding a natural sign.

Works Cited

Adorno, Theodor. "Bach Defended against His Devotees." In Adorno, *Prisms*, trans. Samuel Weber and Shierry Weber, pp. 133–46. 1967. Reprint. Cambridge, Mass.: M.I.T. Press, 1981.

Ahle, Johann Georg. *Kurze doch deutliche Anleitung zu der lieblich- und löblichen Singekunst.* Mühlhausen, 1690.

Aland, Kurt. *Hilfsbuch zum Lutherstudium.* Rev. ed. Witten: Luther-Verlag, 1970.

Althaus, Paul. *The Theology of Martin Luther.* Trans. Robert C. Schultz. Philadelphia: Fortress Press, 1966.

Ansehl, Peter. "Genesis, Wesen, Weiterwirken: Miszellen zur Vivaldischen Ritornellform." *Informazioni e Studi Vivaldiani* 6 (1985): 74–85.

———. "Zum Problem der Ritorncllstrukturen in den Brandenburgischen Konzerten von Johann Sebastian Bach." *Cöthener Bach-Hefte* 4 (1986): 96–100.

Anthony, James R. *French Baroque Music from Beaujoyeulx to Rameau.* Rev. ed. New York: Norton, 1978.

Attali, Jacques. *Noise: The Political Economy of Music.* Trans. Brian Massumi. Minneapolis: University of Minnesota Press, 1985.

Beißwenger, Kirsten. *Johann Sebastian Bachs Notenbibliothek.* Kassel: Bärenreiter, 1992.

Besseler, Heinrich, ed. Johann Sebastian Bach, *Neue Ausgabe sämtlicher Werke.* Vol. 7, part 2: *Sechs Brandenburgische Konzerte.* Kritischer Bericht. Kassel: Bärenreiter, 1956.

———. "Zur Chronologie der Konzerte Joh. Seb. Bachs." In *Festschrift Max Schneider zum achtzigsten Geburtstag*, ed. Walther Vetter, pp. 115–28. Leipzig: VEB Deutscher Verlag für Musik, 1955.

Bloom, Harold. *The Anxiety of Influence: A Theory of Poetry.* London: Oxford University Press, 1973.

Boyd, Malcolm. *Bach: The Brandenburg Concertos.* Cambridge: Cambridge University Press, 1993.

Boyden, David. *The History of Violin Playing, from Its Origins to 1761, and Its Relationship to the Violin and Violin Music.* London: Oxford University Press, 1965.

———. "When Is a Concerto Not a Concerto?" *Musical Quarterly* 43 (1957): 220–32.

Braun, Werner. "The 'Hautboist': An Outline of Evolving Careers and Functions." In *The Social Status of the Professional Musician from the Middle Ages to the Nineteenth Century*, ed. Walter Salmen, pp. 123–58. New York: Pendragon Press, 1983.

Carrell, Norman. *Bach's "Brandenburg Concertos."* London: Allen and Unwin, 1963.

Chafe, Eric. "Allegorical Music: The 'Symbolism' of Tonal Language in the Bach Canons." *Journal of Musicology* 3 (1984): 340–62.

———. "J. S. Bach's *St. Matthew Passion*: Aspects of Planning, Structure, and Chronology." *Journal of the American Musicological Society* 35 (1982): 49–114.

———. "Key Structure and Tonal Allegory in the Passions of J. S. Bach: An Introduction." *Current Musicology* 31 (1981): 39–54.

———. *Tonal Allegory in the Vocal Music of J. S. Bach.* Berkeley and Los Angeles: University of California Press, 1991.

Cox, Howard H. "Bach's Conception of His Office." *Bach* (the journal of the Riemenschneider Bach Institute) 20, no. 1 (1989): 22–30.

———, ed. *The Calov Bible of J. S. Bach.* Ann Arbor: UMI Research Press, 1985.

Dadelsen, Georg von. *Beiträge zur Chronologie der Werke Johann Sebastian Bachs.* Trossingen: Hohner-Verlag, 1958.

Dahlhaus, Carl. "Bachs konzertante Fugen." *Bach-Jahrbuch* 42 (1955): 45–72.

David, Hans T., and Arthur Mendel, eds. *The Bach Reader: A Life of Johann Sebastian Bach in Letters and Documents.* Rev. ed. New York: Norton, 1966.

Degen, Dietz. *Zur Geschichte der Blockflöte in den germanischen Ländern.* Kassel: Bärenreiter, 1936.

Dreyfus, Laurence. *Bach's Continuo Group: Players and Practices in His Vocal Works.* Cambridge, Mass.: Harvard University Press, 1987.

———. "J. S. Bach's Concerto Ritornellos and the Question of Invention." *Musical Quarterly* 71 (1985): 327–58.

———, ed., *Joh. Seb. Bach: Drei Sonaten für Viola da Gamba und Cembalo BWV 1027–1029.* "Concluding Remarks." Leipzig: Peters, 1985.

Drummond, Pippa. *The German Concerto: Five Eighteenth-Century Studies.* Oxford: Oxford University Press, 1980.

Dürr, Alfred, ed. Johann Sebastian Bach, *Neue Ausgabe sämtlicher Werke.* *Nachtrag* to vol. 7, part 2: *Fünftes Brandenburgisches Konzert: Frühfassung BWV 1050a.* Ergänzende Angaben zum Kritischen Bericht, vol. 7, part 2. Kassel: Bärenreiter, 1975.

———, ed. Johann Sebastian Bach, *Neue Ausgabe sämtlicher Werke.* Vol. 1, part 35: *Festmusiken für die Fürstenhäuser von Weimar, Weißenfels und Köthen.* Kritischer Bericht. Kassel: Bärenreiter, 1964.

———. *Die Kantaten von Johann Sebastian Bach.* Rev. ed. Kassel: Bärenreiter, 1985.

————. *Studien über die frühen Kantaten Johann Sebastian Bachs: Verbesserte und erweiterte Fassung der im Jahr 1951 erschienenen Dissertation.* Wiesbaden: Breitkopf and Härtel, 1977.

————. "Zur Entstehungsgeschichte des 5. Brandenburgischen Konzerts." *Bach-Jahrbuch* 61 (1975): 63–69.

————. *Zur Frühgeschichte des Wohltemperierten Klaviers I von Johann Sebastian Bach.* Göttingen: Vandenhoeck and Ruprecht, 1984.

Eggebrecht, Hans Heinrich. "Walthers Musikalisches Lexicon in seiner terminologischen Partien." *Acta Musicologica* 29 (1957): 10–27.

Elias, Norbert. *The Court Society.* Trans. Edmund Jephcott. New York: Pantheon, 1983.

————. *The History of Manners* (vol. 1 of *The Civilizing Process*). Trans. Edmund Jephcott. New York: Pantheon, 1978.

Eller, Rudolf. "Einführungen in die Werke des 38. Deutschen Bachfestes: Die Orchester- und Kammermusikwerke." In *38. Deutsches Bachfest der Neuen Bach-Gesellschaft vom 21. bis 26. Juni 1962 in Leipzig: Bach-Fest-Buch*, pp. 71–96. Leipzig, 1962.

————. "Serie und Zyklus in Bachs Instrumentalsammlungen." In *Bach-Interpretationen: Walter Blankenburg zum 65. Geburtstag*, ed. Martin Geck, pp. 126–43, 221–22. Göttingen: Vandenhoeck and Ruprecht, 1969.

————. "Vivaldi and Bach." In Studi di Musica Veneta Quaderni Vivaldiana, vol. 1: *Vivaldi Veneziano Europeo*, ed. Francesco Degrada, pp. 55–66. Florence: Olschki, 1980.

Finke-Hecklinger, Doris. *Tanzcharaktere in Johann Sebastian Bachs Vokalmusik.* Trossingen: Hohner, 1970.

Fischer, Wilhelm. "Zur Entwicklungsgeschichte des Wiener klassischen Stils." *Studien zur Musikwissenschaft* 3 (1915): 24–84.

Fitzpatrick, Horace. *The Horn and Horn-Playing and the Austro-Bohemian Tradition from 1680–1830.* London: Oxford University Press, 1970.

Fleming, Hanns Friedrich von. *Der vollkommene Teutsche Jäger.* Vol. 1. Leipzig, 1719.

Forkel, Johann Nikolaus. *Über Johann Sebastian Bachs Leben, Kunst und Kunstwerk.* Leipzig, 1802. Reprint, ed. Walther Vetter. Berlin: Henschel, 1966.

Fuller-Maitland, John Alexander. *Bach's "Brandenburg" Concertos.* London: Oxford University Press, 1929.

Geck, Martin. "Gattungstraditionen und Altersschichten in den Brandenburgischen Konzerten." *Die Musikforschung* 23 (1970): 139–52.

Gerber, Rudolph. *Bachs Brandenburgische Konzerte: Eine Einführung in ihre formale und geistige Wesensart.* Kassel: Bärenreiter, 1951.

Goebel, Reinhard. "J. S. Bach: Die Brandenburgischen Konzerte." *Concerto*, no. 8 (1987): 16–18; no. 9 (1987): 10–11.

Goehr, Lydia. *The Imaginary Museum of Musical Works: An Essay in the Philosophy of Music.* Oxford: Clarendon Press, 1992.

Griesinger, Georg August. *Biographische Notizen über Joseph Haydn.* Leipzig, 1810. Trans. Vernon Gotwals in *Haydn: Two Contemporary Portraits,* pp. 3–66. Madison: University of Wisconsin Press, 1968.

Haller, Klaus. *Partituranordnung und musikalischer Satz.* Tutzing: Schneider, 1970.

Hawkins, John. *A General History of the Science and Practice of Music: A New Edition, with the Author's Posthumous Notes.* Vol. 2. London, 1875.

Heller, Karl, ed. Johann Sebastian Bach, *Neue Ausgabe sämtlicher Werke,* vol. 4, part 8: *Bearbeitungen fremder Werke.* Kritischer Bericht. Kassel: Bärenreiter, 1980.

Herz, Gerhard. "J. S. Bach 1733: A 'New' Bach Signature." In *Studies in Renaissance and Baroque Music in Honor of Arthur Mendel,* ed. Robert L. Marshall, pp. 255–63. Kassel: Bärenreiter, 1974.

Hiller, Johann Adam. *Lebensbeschreibungen berühmter Musikgelehrten und Tonkünstler, neuerer Zeit.* Leipzig, 1784.

Hoppe, Günther. "Köthener politische, ökonomische und höfische Verhältnisse als Schaffensbedingungen Bachs (Teil 1)." *Cöthener Bach-Hefte* 4 (1986): 13–62.

Hosler, Bellamy. *Changing Aesthetic Views of Instrumental Music in Eighteenth-Century Germany.* Ann Arbor: UMI Research Press, 1981.

Hunt, Edgar. *The Recorder and Its Music.* Rev. ed. London: Eulenburg, 1977.

Hutchings, Arthur. *The Baroque Concerto.* Rev. ed. London: Faber, 1973.

Irwin, Joyce. "Music and the Doctrine of Adiaphora in Orthodox Lutheran Theology." *Sixteenth Century Journal* 14 (1983): 157–72.

Kirkendale, Ursula. "The Source for Bach's *Musical Offering*: The *Institutio oratoria* of Quintilian." *Journal of the American Musicological Society* 33 (1980): 88–141.

Klein, Hans-Günter. *Der Einfluß der Vivaldischen Konzertform im Instrumentalwerk Johann Sebastian Bachs.* Strasbourg: Heitz, 1970.

Kobayashi, Yoshitake. "Diplomatische Überlegungen zur Chronologie der Weimarer Vokalwerke." Paper delivered at the Bach-Kolloquium Rostock, 1990.

Koch, Ernst. "Tröstendes Echo: Zur theologischen Deutung der Echo-Arie im IV. Teil des Weihnachts-Oratoriums von Johann Sebastian Bach." *Bach-Jahrbuch* 75 (1989): 203–11.

Krey, Johannes. "Zur Entstehungsgeschichte des ersten Brandenburgischen Konzerts." In *Festschrift Heinrich Besseler zum sechzigsten Geburtstag,* ed. Institut für Musikwissenschaft der Karl-Marx-Universität, pp. 337–42. Leipzig: VEB Deutscher Verlag für Musik, 1961.

Kross, Siegfried. "Concerto—Concertare und Conserere." In *Bericht über den internationalen musikwissenschaftlichen Kongreß Leipzig 1966*, ed. Carl Dahlhaus, pp. 216–20. Kassel: Bärenreiter, 1970.

Kubitschek, Ernst. "Block- und Querflöte im Umkreis von J. J. Fux: Versuch einer Übersicht." In *Johann Joseph Fux und die barocke Bläsertradition: Kongreßbericht Graz 1985*, ed. Bernhard Habla, pp. 99–119. Tutzing: Schneider, 1987.

Kusko, Bruce. "Proton Milloprobe Analysis of the Hand-Penned Annotations in Bach's Calov Bible." In *The Calov Bible of J. S. Bach*, ed. Howard H. Cox, pp. 31–106. Ann Arbor: UMI Research Press, 1985.

Landmann, Ortrun. "The Dresden Hofkapelle during the Lifetime of Johann Sebastian Bach." *Early Music* 17 (1989): 17–30.

———. "Einige Überlegungen zu den Konzerten 'nebenamtlich' komponierender Dresdener Hofmusiker in der Zeit von etwa 1715 bis 1763." In Studien zur Aufführungspraxis und Interpretation von Instrumentalmusik des 18. Jahrhunderts, Heft 20, *Die Entwicklung des Solokonzerts im 18. Jahrhundert*, ed. Eitelfriedrich Thom, pp. 57–73. Michaelstein/Blankenburg, 1983.

Lang-Becker, Elke. *Johann Sebastian Bach: Die Brandenburgischen Konzerte*. Munich: Fink, 1990.

Leaver, Robin A. *Bachs Theologische Bibliothek: Eine kritische Bibliographie*. Neuhaussen-Stuttgart: Hänssler, 1983.

———. *J. S. Bach and Scripture: Glosses from the Calov Bible Commentary*. St. Louis: Concordia, 1985.

Leavis Ralph. "J. S. Bach's Violone Parts." *Galpin Society Journal* 30 (1977): 155–56.

Leppert, Richard. "Music, Representation, and Social Order in Early-Modern Europe." *Cultural Critique* 12 (1989): 25–55.

Lester, Joel. *Between Modes and Keys: German Theory, 1592–1802*. Stuyvesant, N.Y.: Pendragon Press, 1989.

———. "Major-Minor Concepts and Modal Theory in Germany, 1592–1680." *Journal of the American Musicological Society* 30 (1977): 208–53.

———. "The Recognition of Major and Minor Keys in German Theory: 1680–1730." *Journal of Music Theory* 22 (1978): 65–103.

Little, Meredith Ellis. "Minuet." In *The New Grove Dictionary of Music and Musicians*, ed. Stanley Sadie, vol. 12, pp. 353–58. London: Macmillan, 1980.

Luther, Martin. *Lectures on Deuteronomy*. Trans. Richard R. Caemmerer, ed. Jaroslav Pelikan. Vol. 9 of *Luther's Works*. St. Louis: Concordia, 1960.

———. *The Magnificat*. Trans. A.T.W. Steinhaeuser, ed. Jaroslav Pelikan. Vol. 21 of *Luther's Works*, pp. 295–355. St. Louis: Concordia, 1956.

———. "On Secular Authority." In *Luther and Calvin on Secular Authority*, trans. and ed. Harro Hopfl. Cambridge: Cambridge University Press, 1991.

Marissen, Michael. "Bach-Repertoire für Flötisten." *Tibia* 12 (1987): 537–40.

―――. "Beziehungen zwischen der Besetzung und dem Satzaufbau im ersten Satz des sechsten Brandenburgischen Konzerts von Johann Sebastian Bach." *Beiträge zur Bach-Forschung* 9–10 (1991): 104–28.

―――. "Concerto Styles and Signification in Bach's First Brandenburg Concerto." Forthcoming in *Bach Perspectives* 1 (1995).

―――. "A Critical Reappraisal of J. S. Bach's A-Major Flute Sonata." *Journal of Musicology* 6 (1988): 367–86.

―――. "J. S. Bach's Brandenburg Concertos as a Meaningful Set." *Musical Quarterly* 77 (1993): 193–235.

―――, and Daniel Melamed. *J. S. Bach: A Guide to Research.* New York: Garland, forthcoming.

―――. "More Source-Critical Research on J. S. Bach's *Musical Offering.*" *Bach* (the journal of the Riemenschneider Bach Institute) 25, no. 1 (1994): 11–27.

―――. "On Linking Bach's F-Major Sinfonia and His Hunt Cantata." *Bach* (the journal of the Riemenschneider Bach Institute) 23, no. 2 (1992): 31–46.

―――. "Organological Questions and Their Significance in J. S. Bach's Fourth Brandenburg Concerto." *Journal of the American Musical Instrument Society* 17 (1991): 5–52.

―――. "Performance Practice Issues that Affect Meaning in Selected Bach Instrumental Works." In *Perspectives on Bach Performance,* ed. Robin Stowell. Cambridge: Cambridge University Press, forthcoming.

―――. "Relationships between Scoring and Structure in the First Movement of Bach's Sixth Brandenburg Concerto." *Music and Letters* 71 (1990): 494–504.

―――. "Religious Aims in Mendelssohn's 1829 Berlin-Singakademie Performances of Bach's St. Matthew Passion." *Musical Quarterly* 77 (1993): 718–26.

―――. "The Theological Character of J. S. Bach's *Musical Offering.*" *Bach-Studies* 2, ed. Daniel Melamed. Cambridge: Cambridge University Press, forthcoming.

―――. "A Trio in C Major for Recorder, Violin and Continuo by J. S. Bach?" *Early Music* 13 (1985): 384–90.

Marshall, Robert L. *The Compositional Process of J. S. Bach: A Study of the Autograph Scores of the Vocal Works.* Princeton: Princeton University Press, 1972.

―――. *The Music of Johann Sebastian Bach: The Sources, the Style, the Significance.* New York: Schirmer, 1989.

―――. "Tempo and Dynamic Indications in the Bach Sources: A Review of the Terminology." In *Bach, Händel, Scarlatti: Tercentenary Essays,* ed. Peter Williams, pp. 259–75. Cambridge: Cambridge University Press, 1985.

Mattheson, Johann. *Grundlage einer Ehren-Pforte*. Hamburg, 1740.

———. *Das Neu-eröffnete Orchestre*. Hamburg, 1713.

———. *Der musicalische Patriot*. Hamburg, 1728.

———. *Der vollkommene Capellmeister*. Hamburg, 1739.

Maunder, Richard. "The Violone in Bach's Brandenburg Concerti." *Galpin Society Journal* 31 (1978): 147.

McClary, Susan. "The Blasphemy of Talking Politics during Bach Year." In *Music and Society: The Politics of Composition, Performance and Reception*, ed. Richard Leppert and Susan McClary, pp. 13–62. Cambridge: Cambridge University Press, 1987.

Melamed, Daniel, and Michael Marissen. *J. S. Bach: A Guide to Research*. New York: Garland, forthcoming.

Mendel, Arthur, and Hans T. David, eds. *The Bach Reader: A Life of Johann Sebastian Bach in Letters and Documents*. Rev. ed. New York: Norton, 1966.

Moser, Andreas. "Der Violino piccolo." *Zeitschrift für Musikwissenschaft* 1 (1918–19): 377–80.

Nestle, Rosemarie. "Das Bachschriftum 1981–1985." *Bach-Jahrbuch* 75 (1989): 107–89.

Neumann, Werner, and Hans-Joachim Schulze, eds. *Bach-Dokumente I: Schriftstücke von der Hand Johann Sebastian Bachs*. Kassel: Bärenreiter, 1963.

———. *Bach-Dokumente II: Fremdschriftliche und gedruckte Dokumente zum Lebensgeschichte Johann Sebastian Bachs 1685–1750*. Kassel: Bärenreiter, 1969.

Ottenberg, Hans-Günter. *C.P.E. Bach*. Oxford: Oxford University Press, 1987.

Petzoldt, Richard. *Georg Philipp Telemann*. Trans. Horace Fitzpatrick. New York: Oxford University Press, 1974.

Prinz, Ulrich. "Studien zum Instrumentarium Johann Sebastian Bachs mit besonderer Berücksichtigung der Kantaten." Ph.D. dissertation, Tübingen University, 1979.

Quantz, Johann Joachim. *On Playing the Flute*. Rev. ed. Trans. and ed. Edward R. Reilly. New York: Schirmer, 1985.

———. *Versuch einer Anweisung die Flöte traversiere zu spielen*. Berlin, 1752.

Rackwitz, Werner, ed. *Georg Philipp Telemann: Singen ist das Fundament zur Music in allen Dingen—Eine Dokumentensammlung*. Leipzig: Philipp Reclam jun., 1981.

Rameau, Jean-Philippe. *Traité de l'Harmonie*. Paris, 1722.

Reichardt, Johann Friedrich. "Autobiographie." *Allgemeine musikalische Zeitung* 16 (1814): 29.

Reimer, Erich. "Concerto/Konzert." 1973. In *Handwörterbuch der musikalischen Terminologie*, ed. Hans Heinrich Eggebrecht. Wiesbaden: F. Steiner, 1972–.

Rust, Wilhelm, ed. *Joh. Seb. Bachs Werke: Gesamtausgabe der Bachgesellschaft*. Vol. 19: *Kammermusik, Dritter Band*. Leipzig, 1869.

Ryom, Peter. *Répertoire des Oeuvres d'Antonio Vivaldi: Les compositions instrumentales.* Copenhagen: Engstrøm and Sødring, 1986.

Sachs, Klaus-Jürgen. "Aspekte der numerischen und tonartlichen Disposition instrumentalmusikalischer Zyklen des ausgehenden 17. und beginnenden 18. Jahrhunderts." *Archiv für Musikwissenschaft* 41 (1984): 237–56.

Sackmann, Dominik. "Toccata F-dur (BWV 540)—eine analytische Studie." In *Bericht über die wissenschaftliche Konferenz zum 5. Internationalen Bachfest der DDR,* ed. Winfried Hoffmann and Armin Schneiderheinze, pp. 351–60. Leipzig: VEB Deutscher Verlag für Musik, 1988.

Scherliess, Volker. "Musica Politica." In *Festschrift Georg von Dadelsen zum 60. Geburtstag,* ed. Thomas Kohlhase and Volker Scherliess, pp. 270–83. Neuhausen-Stuttgart: Hänssler, 1978.

Schmidt, Harro. "Die Viola da gamba der Violinfamilie: Ein vergessener Gambentyp des Barock." In *Alte Musik als ästhetische Gegenwart: Kongreßbericht Stuttgart 1985,* ed. Dietrich Berke and Dorothee Hanemann, vol. 2, pp. 422–26. Kassel: Bärenreiter, 1987.

Schulze, Hans-Joachim, and Werner Neumann, eds. *Bach-Dokumente I: Schriftstücke von der Hand Johann Sebastian Bachs.* Kassel: Bärenreiter, 1963.

———. *Bach-Dokumente II: Fremdschriftliche und gedruckte Dokumente zum Lebensgeschichte Johann Sebastian Bachs 1685–1750.* Kassel: Bärenreiter, 1969.

Schulze, Hans-Joachim, ed. *Bach-Dokumente III: Dokumente zum Nachwirken Johann Sebastian Bachs 1750–1800.* Kassel: Bärenreiter, 1972.

———. "J. S. Bach's Concerto-Arrangements for Organ—Studies or Commissioned Works?" *Organ Yearbook* 3 (1972): 4–13.

———, ed. *Johann Sebastian Bach: Leben und Werk in Dokumenten.* Leipzig: VEB Deutscher Taschenbuch Verlag, 1975.

———. "Johann Sebastian Bachs Konzertbearbeitungen nach Vivaldi und anderen—Studien- oder Auftragswerke?" *Deutsches Jahrbuch der Musikwissenschaft* 18 (1978): 80–100.

———. "Johann Sebastian Bachs Konzerte—Fragen der Überlieferung und Chronologie." In Bach-Studien 6, *Beiträge zum Konzertschaffen Johann Sebastian Bachs,* ed. Peter Ansehl, pp. 9–26. Leipzig: VEB Breitkopf and Härtel, 1981.

———. *Studien zur Bach-Überlieferung im 18. Jahrhundert.* Leipzig: Peters, 1984.

Siegele, Ulrich. *Kompositionsweise und Bearbeitungstechnik in der Instrumentalmusik Johann Sebastian Bachs.* Neuhausen-Stuttgart: Hänssler, 1975.

Smend, Friedrich. *Bach in Köthen.* Berlin: Christlicher Zeitschriftenverlag, 1951. Trans. John Page, ed. and rev. Stephen Daw. St. Louis: Concordia, 1985.

Spalding, Keith. *An Historical Dictionary of German Figurative Usage.* Oxford: Blackwell, 1952–.

Spitta, Philipp. *Johann Sebastian Bach.* Leipzig, 1873–80.

———. *Johann Sebastian Bach: His Work and Influence on the Music of Germany.* Vol. 2. Trans. Clara Bell and J. A. Fuller-Maitland. London, 1889.

Spitzer, John. "Speaking of Orchestras." Paper delivered 5 November 1993 at the national meeting of the American Musicological Society, Montreal.

Stauffer, George. "Bach as Reviser of His Own Keyboard Works." *Early Music* 13 (1985): 185–98.

———. *The Organ Preludes of Johann Sebastian Bach.* Ann Arbor: UMI Research Press, 1980.

Stinson, Russell. *The Bach Manuscripts of Johann Peter Kellner and His Circle.* Durham, N.C.: Duke University Press, 1989.

———. "The 'Critischer Musicus' as Keyboard Transcriber? Scheibe, Bach, and Vivaldi." *Journal of Musicological Research* 9 (1990): 255–71.

———. "J. P. Kellner's Copy of Bach's Sonatas and Partitas for Violin Solo." *Early Music* 13 (1985): 199–211.

Talbot, Michael. "The Concerto Allegro in the Early Eighteenth Century." *Music and Letters* 52 (1971): 8–18, 159–72.

———. *Vivaldi.* Rev. ed. New York: Schirmer, 1993.

———. "Vivaldi and Rome: Observations and Hypotheses." *Journal of the Royal Musical Association* 113 (1988): 28–46.

Tarr, Edward. "Monteverdi, Bach und die Trompetenmusik ihrer Zeit." In *Bericht über den internationalen musikwissenschaftlichen Kongreß Bonn 1970*, ed. Carl Dahlhaus, pp. 592–96. Kassel: Bärenreiter, 1971.

Taruskin, Richard. "The Pastness of the Present and the Presence of the Past." In *Authenticity and Early Music: A Symposium*, ed. Nicholas Kenyon, pp. 137–210. Oxford: Oxford University Press, 1988.

Terry, Charles Sanford. *Bach's Orchestra.* London: Oxford University Press, 1932.

Tobin, John, ed. *Georg Friedrich Händel: The Messiah.* Leipzig: VEB Deutscher Verlag für Musik, 1968.

Tripp, Paul. *Tubby the Tuba.* Produced and directed by George Pal. Hollywood: Paramount Pictures, 1946.

Vester, Frans. *Flute Music of the Eighteenth Century: An Annotated Bibliography.* Monteux: Musica Rara, 1985.

Wackernagel, Peter. "Beobachten am Autograph von Bachs Brandenburgischen Konzerten." In *Festschrift Max Schneider zum achtzigsten Geburtstag*, ed. Walther Vetter, pp. 129–38. Leipzig: VEB Deutscher Verlag für Musik, 1955.

———. *Johann Sebastian Bach: Brandenburgische Konzerte.* Berlin: Bote and Bock, 1938.

———, ed. *J. S. Bach, Brandenburgische Konzerte: Faksimile nach dem im Besitz der Staatsbibliothek in Berlin befindlichen Autograph.* Leipzig: Peters, 1947.

Weber, Max. *The Protestant Ethic and the Spirit of Capitalism.* Trans. Talcott Parsons. New York: Scribner's, 1958.

Whaples, Miriam K. "Bach's Earliest Arias." *Bach* (the journal of the Riemenschneider Bach Institute) 20, no. 1 (1989): 31–54.

Whitmore, Philip. "Towards an Understanding of the Capriccio." *Journal of the Royal Musical Association* 113 (1988): 47–56.

———. *Unpremeditated Art: The Cadenza in the Classical Keyboard Concerto.* Oxford: Clarendon Press, 1991.

Williams, Peter. *The Organ Music of J. S. Bach.* Vol. 1. Cambridge: Cambridge University Press, 1980.

Wolff, Christoph, ed. *Bach-Bibliographie.* Kassel: Merseburger, 1985.

———. *Bach: Essays on His Life and Music.* Cambridge, Mass.: Harvard University Press, 1991.

———. *The New Grove Bach Family.* New York: Norton, 1983.

———. "New Research on Bach's *Musical Offering.*" *Musical Quarterly* 57 (1971): 379–408.

———. "Die Rastrierungen in den Originalhandschriften Johann Sebastian Bachs und ihre Bedeutung für die diplomatische Quellenkritik." In *Festschrift für Friedrich Smend zum 70. Geburtstag,* pp. 80–92. Berlin: Merseburger, 1963.

———. "Vivaldi's Compositional Art, Bach, and the Process of 'Musical Thinking.'" In Wolff, *Bach: Essays on His Life and Music,* pp. 72–83. Cambridge, Mass.: Harvard University Press, 1991.

———. "Zur Chronologie und Kompositionsgeschichte von Bachs Kunst der Fuge." *Beiträge zur Musikwissenschaft* 25 (1983): 130–42.

Wolschke, Martin. *Von der Stadtpfeiferei zur Lehrlingskapelle und Sinfonieorchester.* Regensburg: Bosse, 1981.

Woodfield, Ian. *The Early History of the Viol.* Cambridge: Cambridge University Press, 1984.

Zimpel, Herbert. "In der Köthener Stadtpfeiferakte geblättert." *Cöthener Bach-Hefte* 3 (1985): 65–71.

✤ *Index* ✤

BACH'S WORKS

Bach's Works by BWV Number

RELATED NAMES AND SUBJECTS